What people are saying about …

MESSY CHURCH

"The title of Ross's carefully thought-out book is catchy, but make no mistake. There's nothing 'messy' about his life, heart, or ministry. The practicality of his leadership is verifiable, his integrity reliable, his credibility certifiable, and his heart for God clearly manifest in his worship ministry and leadership."

Jack Hayford, chancellor of
The King's University, Los Angeles

"When Ross Parsley writes about the local church, we all should read it. He is one of the brightest young pastors in our nation and a true friend in the ministry."

Brady Boyd, pastor of New Life Church
in Colorado Springs, Colorado

"*Messy Church* is a living and divine philosophical underpinning upon which many can stand. It speaks of relationship with God. I hear the Father speaking through Ross into the storm of people rushing to fulfill their calling in the kingdom of God. This is a clear reflection of what God is indeed saying to the church in these days. Basically this: His kingdom is to be based upon relationship, rather than on authority."

Britt Hancock, church planter and
founder of Mountain Gateway

"Messy Church will literally mess you up, but in a good way. I love how Ross Parsley is able to showcase a concept that often takes us down a negative, critical road and instead highlights the hope, life, restoration, and purpose we can find in spiritual family. He truly helps us to see that through the good, the bad, and the ugly, family is still family. Not only will your perspective change, but you will put this down and walk away with tons of practical ways to create a culture of spiritual family that everyone needs."

Dino Rizzo, lead pastor of Healing Place
Church in Baton Rouge, Louisiana,
and author of *Servolution*

"With powerful insight, personal experience, and refreshing transparency, Ross reveals a message needed to make your spiritual journey make sense. Allow the Holy Spirit to challenge and inspire you as you begin to understand the kind of church God uses—*Messy Church.*"

Chris Hodges, senior pastor of Church
of the Highlands in Birmingham,
Alabama, and author of *Fresh Air*

"Ross combines life lessons shaped by profound experience with a delightfully conversational style of communication to bring to us a message that is both significant in substance and enjoyable in style. In a day when ecclesiology (our theology about the church) is being reinvented, we need books like this that hold us to the center. A profitable read!"

Bob Sorge, author, www.oasishouse.com

MESSY CHURCH

MESSY
CHURCH

a multigenerational
mission for God's family

ROSS
PARSLEY

David C Cook®
transforming lives together

MESSY CHURCH
Published by David C Cook
4050 Lee Vance View
Colorado Springs, CO 80918 U.S.A.

David C Cook Distribution Canada
55 Woodslee Avenue, Paris, Ontario, Canada N3L 3E5

David C Cook U.K., Kingsway Communications
Eastbourne, East Sussex BN23 6NT, England

The graphic circle C logo is a registered trademark of David C Cook.

The website addresses recommended throughout this book are offered as a
resource to you. These websites are not intended in any way to be or imply an
endorsement on the part of David C Cook, nor do we vouch for their content.

Unless otherwise noted, all Scripture quotations are taken from the Holy
Bible, New International Version®, NIV®. Copyright © 1973, 2011 by Biblica,
Inc.™ Used by permission of Zondervan. All rights reserved worldwide. www.
zondervan.com. Scripture quotations marked ESV are taken from The Holy Bible,
English Standard Version® (ESV®), copyright © 2001 by Crossway, a publishing
ministry of Good News Publishers. Used by permission. All rights reserved;
KJV are taken from the King James Version of the Bible. (Public Domain.)

LCCN 2012936139
ISBN 978-1-4347-9937-1
eISBN 978-1-4347-0506-8

© 2012 Ross Parsley

The Team: John Blase, Alex Field, Nick Lee, Renada Arens, Karen Athen
Cover Design: Amy Konyndyk
Cover Photo: iStockphoto

Printed in the United States of America
First Edition 2012

1 2 3 4 5 6 7 8 9 10

042712

This book is dedicated to my family:

My original family—who taught me the most valuable lessons of life.

Growing up as a Parsley has been a wonderful and God-filled journey. Dad and Mom, you instilled in me the values and character traits that have allowed me to make it through even the most difficult moments of life. And what the Enemy meant for evil in our lives, God has turned into something beautiful for us all.

My blended family—who taught me all about grace.

At nineteen years old I embarked on a great adventure with all of you as our families merged into one. The power of a second chance came alive to me in the strength of our new experience. Loud, boisterous, full of life and energy, our house full of teenagers was crazy. But we will never forget the pivotal and shaping memories of God's grace for us all.

My immediate family—who continues to teach me how to love.

Aimee, you are the love of my life and God's greatest gift to me. You are my compass and courage, always protecting, always serving. You make our family what it is. Zachary, Taylor, Grace, Ethan, and Owen, you are my joy and crown. I'm so proud of each of you and can't wait to see how God continues to use each of you in His great plan.

My ONEchapel family—who is teaching me how to live by faith.

Our journey is not yet long enough to know what God will do with us in this city, but I am so grateful for a group of people who love so easily, connect so willingly, and believe so faithfully. The best is yet to come for us, and that's saying something because it has been an amazing ride so far. Thank you for increasing my faith in how Jesus builds His church!

ACKNOWLEDGMENTS

It seems to me as if writing a book is the result of a massive amount of investments by all kinds of people. I know that I am the author but not the only writer. As a family produces offspring and then contributes to each individual's experience, so I have many thanks to give and several acknowledgments to offer in producing this little book.

Thank you to Don Pape, who believed in this book long before I had the capacity to produce it. I'm grateful for your confidence.

Thank you to Alex Field, my editor, who grew in the virtue of patience this last year because of me. I appreciate your encouragement and direction in getting this book done.

Thank you to Rob Stennett, who challenged me to keep telling my stories. You made this book more interesting.

Thank you to my New Life Church family, who allowed me to learn many of the lessons contained in this book. You will always be a miracle to me.

Thank you to Glenn Packiam, Jared Anderson, and John Egan, specifically, who had to endure these lessons up close. You were the instruments God used to speak into my life about the generations.

Thank you, God, our heavenly Father, for making us all part of your family.

CONTENTS

FOREWORD

One time, when I was visiting a church as a guest speaker, the pastor said to me, "Thank you for coming with a clean screen." Confused, I asked him, "What do you mean?" He told me he viewed people as window screens. When you wash a window screen with a water hose, whatever is in the screen will come out the other side, no matter how pure the water is. He said, "When some ministers come teach at our church, it feels like God's words are filtered through too much of their own agenda."

I've never forgotten that.

The first time I met Ross Parsley, I thought, *Here's a man with a clean screen.* At the time, Ross was guiding New Life Church in Colorado Springs through a troubled and difficult season. When New Life's senior pastor stepped down due to a moral failure, Ross stepped in as interim pastor, and he did an incredible job.

Because of the unique perspective God has given him on the church, I'm convinced Ross is the only person who could have successfully guided New Life through that storm. As you will learn in this book, Ross believes a church (and *the* Church) should operate like a family. He didn't see New Life as a machine that needed to be fixed, but as a hurting family in need of healing. With a true father's heart, he put the best interest of his church family ahead of his own.

When the New Life search committee was considering Brady Boyd, a Gateway pastor, as a candidate to become their new senior pastor, we told them, "If you say yes to Brady, you're also saying yes to his church family." Brady spent years as a pastor here at Gateway and also had a strong relationship with pastor Jimmy Evans and Trinity Fellowship in Amarillo, Texas. After the search committee selected Brady, they told us this family attitude was one of the determining factors. They knew they had found a great man of God in Brady as well as a whole new family in Gateway and Trinity. They wanted to "marry" Brady *and* build relationship with us … the in-laws!

I was blown away by Ross's supportive attitude. Not only had he served as interim pastor, but he had also been a candidate for the permanent position. When the search committee announced their choice, Ross didn't fight their decision or treat Brady with hostility. He received his new family, faithfully serving as Brady's right-hand man, even while the Holy Spirit was giving him the desire to plant a church. When the time came for Ross to launch out and plant ONEchapel in Austin, the Lord honored his heart. It's amazing to see what God is doing through Ross and his new family.

Clearly, when Ross writes about treating the church like a true family, in good times and bad, he writes from experience. He's lived it. He has proven time and time again that his main priority is the well-being of God's family. He has lived by the principles found in this book, even when it has been inconvenient for him. I encourage you to listen to the truth God has given Ross. I can't think of anyone better to communicate God's heart for His bride than Ross Parsley—a true "clean screen."

Robert Morris

Founding senior pastor, Gateway Church

Best-selling author of *The Blessed Life, From Dream to Destiny,* and *The God I Never Knew*

INTRODUCTION: A BEAUTIFUL MESS

The whimpering started first—just an annoying sound coming from down the hall through the darkness. Surprisingly, I woke up first even though I usually sleep like a rock. Lying still, I secretly hoped my wife would hear the crying and make the trek down the hall to comfort whoever had begun moaning.

Saturday night always seems restless when you're a pastor with five kids. Someone always wakes up. Funny how it never seems to happen on Monday night.

Anyway, the moaning didn't stop; it got louder, turned into a full-scale cry, and finally, a bloodcurdling scream. My youngest sons, Ethan, five, and Owen, three, were crying when I stumbled into their room. Ethan was on the top bunk, holding his stomach, and Owen, on the bottom bunk, crying in fear. As I reached toward Ethan, he leaned over the railing of his bunk bed and threw up, the most I'd ever seen come out of a five-year-old. I jumped out of the way but felt the spray of vomit on my face. Owen screamed, "My eye, Ethan threw up in my eye!" By this time Aimee had arrived and, after a moment of shock, started to laugh.

Into the bath went the boys while I cleaned up the carpet and the beds. What a mess!

Aimee and I have five beautiful children, now ages five to seventeen years old. With seven people living under one roof, things often get messy. The day-to-day routine has a way of piling up around you when this many people share life together. Sometimes two and a half bathrooms don't seem to be enough, and often we set the dinner table with paper plates just to help with the immense cleanup. We have crazy days and sleepless nights, but it's not miserable. Disorganized? Sure. Frustrating? Sometimes. But our family is beautiful. We love each other, and we're finding our rhythm during this season, after moving from Colorado Springs, Colorado, to Austin, Texas, to plant a new church called ONEchapel.

We packed all of our worldly possession into three PODS, sold our house in Colorado, and lived with friends for a month before moving to New Braunfels, Texas (forty-five minutes outside of Austin), to live with Aimee's mom. We spent almost four months looking for a house to rent in Austin and we lived in that rental house for one year. Then, we finally found a lovely house to purchase just around the corner from where we rented.

That's four moves in less than two years.

Did I mention that we planted a church during that time?

We still don't have our pictures hung, and boxes continue to sit in several of our rooms and closets. We go about our days doing a little painting when we can and putting things where we think they should go as we have time.

Our little family of seven has settled into a routine, going to work and school, celebrating birthdays, doing homework, preparing for church on Sunday, fighting over the bathrooms, and generally enjoying life together.

The half-painted walls are the backdrop for our Wednesday-night young-marrieds group. We've invited them, not just into our house, but into our lives as well. This full-of-boxes, half-painted, bare-walled house reflects where we are in our journey and what's going on in our family.

We feel blessed in the middle of our journey. We've cried together, fought through the bad days together, and encouraged one another. The church continues to grow phenomenally, and we're all working to do what God called us to do as a family.

There's peanut butter and jelly smudged on the refrigerator, clothes on the bathroom floor, chips in the couch cushions, and empty milk glasses on the counter. In between middle-school choir concerts, first-grade daddy's day, high-school football games, guitar lessons, pre-school, and late-night talks, we're experiencing a beautiful life together.

It's a bit of a mess … but it's *our mess*.

A beautiful mess!

Families aren't perfect and neither are churches.

Church planting has me thinking a lot about family. In many respects, ONEchapel is an extension of the Parsley family. Our kids are working alongside us, serving in children's ministry, setting up chairs and sound systems, and leading worship or small groups. What's so amazing is to watch our kids embrace the calling that is on our family. Both Aimee and I are pastor's kids, and our parents support and encourage us as we plant this church.

The truth is that in the process, I've had to consider and recon-sider the way we do church. You see, as a pastor I don't want my kids to resent church because it feels more like a job than a family. I don't want to create something synthetic or mechanical. I want our church to be life giving and organic. I want my kids to receive life in the midst of this experience, not just duty. Of course, I know that we can't avoid the struggle or responsibility that automatically comes with relationships. Every family has a set of chores that need to be done, and churches are no different.

But what if I could treat my church like I treat my family? No, not the way I sometimes mistreat my family, but the way I know I should treat my family. What if I had the same love and grace for my church that I have for my own family? What would happen if I had hopes and aspirations for the young people in my church the way I dream of a life for my own children? How would our church be different if we embraced our older members the same way we teach our children to honor their grandparents? What does a multigenerational church actually look like, and how would it interact with our fatherless and orphan culture?

That's what this book is all about. After almost twenty years as a pastor at the influential and storied New Life Church, I've experienced a family church environment in the midst of growth, change, pain, and tragedy. As a worship leader, I witnessed firsthand the need for an intergenerational synergy that fuels worship, drawing in every age to share at a family worship table, teaching us how to value our heritage and at the same time embrace what God is doing now. Growing up in church, sitting in the front row as a pastor's kid, I know what it's like to see the best and worst of the people of God. And now, as a church planter, I'm experiencing what it means to encourage a new family of believers to love one another and share life together—regardless of how messy it is. As a pastor's kid who grew up in small towns being shaped by a small church community, and as part of the inner workings of a megachurch, I have a beautiful story to tell and continue to love pastoring.

This is not a book about how broken people are, although it is true—people are broken and need healing. It is not a book about how messy ministry can be, although it is truly messier than any of us would like. I am not writing out of a cynical or skeptical view of church life. I love the body of Christ and have given most of my life to pastoring and serving people. I believe in the family of God. I'm not interested in talking about the failures of the church, though they may be many; I want to talk about family.

The family of God.

I want to share a paradigm that will change how you engage with your church. I want to highlight the struggles, challenges, and benefits of a multigenerational, interactive family ministry and the strength that lies within a group of people who love one another so deeply that they are willing to lay down their lives for each other. I want to challenge you to think not in terms of years but decades and generations when it comes to your church family. Will it last? Will your church stand the test of time, or will it end up whimpering across the finish line with a few aged saints who were faithful, but who weren't able to translate the gospel message for the next generation?

If you're hungry for something more than a sixty-five-minute church service each week, a service that is perfectly programmed for your emotional needs, then you need a family, not just a nice church. If you're tired of never being able to admit there's a mess in and around your life, you need to find a family instead of a religion. If you want a way to make your community of believers more authentic, connected, and fulfilling, keep reading. I believe it is possible.

Of course, I don't have all the answers, and I certainly don't have five easy steps to transform a fledgling congregation into a growing megachurch. I'm in the process of growing a new, healthy family of believers myself. But I promise that the journey is full of adventure, risk, failure, challenge, and beauty. Just like your family and mine.

It might be a bit more chaotic and disorganized than the church you're used to. It may turn out more muddled and messy than you'd like, but it will be real, authentic, and … healthy.

In fact, I can pretty much guarantee that it will be a mess.

A beautiful mess.

Chapter 1

WAKING UP

"Babe, I think this is it!" Aimee said.

I didn't open my eyes. I was too exhausted. I had been asleep for barely two and a half hours. The stench of yesterday was still on my breath. *Did it really happen? Did I really just walk through that? And what now? What is supposed to happen now?* These questions were clattering around in my brain when I somehow finally drifted to sleep. Yesterday was a day that I never thought would happen, a day that seemed surreal and grainy, like an awful nightmare....

Aimee poked me on the shoulder and said, "Babe, I think this is really it."

I didn't even open my eyes. "No it isn't ..."

"Yes, this is it! Get up and get dressed. We've got to go," she said firmly.

I opened my eyes and looked at the red numbers glowing from my bedside clock radio: 2:06 a.m.

Begrudgingly, I rolled out of my cozy bed and began to get ready to go to the hospital. I should have known better than to doubt my bride of fifteen years. She had already done this four times, and it was clear by now that she knew what labor pain felt like. She was on a mission. Baby number five was not going to deliver without an epidural!

We arrived at the hospital without too much drama, got checked in, and then nurses hooked Aimee up to all the monitors and sensors that accommodate a twenty-first-century birthing center. It was four thirty in the morning, and the soft glow of the birthing room with casual blond-wood furniture became our refuge for the next forty-eight hours. I curled up on the makeshift bed/window bench and pulled a hospital throw blanket up close to my face.

We had just begun, and already I felt emotionally spent. My mind raced. The heaviness in the pit of my stomach was unbearable. Our family was about to change. We would welcome a brand-new baby boy into this world in just a few short hours … and at the moment it seemed like a world of anguish, disappointment, and pain.

It was Friday, November 3, 2006.

Thursday had come like a whirlwind that tore apart our church family with an emotional severity that I had never experienced. A tornado of allegations, rumors, and unbelievable accusations had consumed our thoughts and emotions all day at New Life Church.

I had known since nine thirty that morning that some of the allegations were true, and we were just trying to get our arms around what to do next. I called a staff meeting and said some words that sounded hollow as I tried to bring comfort and strength to a roomful of people in need of assurance.

"We have a process to deal with these kinds of allegations set forth in our bylaws, and the overseers are flying in now to engage …" I was barely present. It was surreal. I felt the out-of-body experience happening to me as I sat in front of our staff on that wooden stool inside the little youth building we called "The Tent." They looked fearful, with empty looks in their eyes as they wondered why I wasn't saying, "This is all nothing to worry about; everybody go back to work."

Later Thursday evening, I attended a trustee meeting where six wise, older men heard the unthinkable. I walked across the parking lot to the next meeting, where our elders had gathered with our church overseers. The cold November wind felt like relief on my warm cheeks. The room was tense when I arrived, and I felt the shock and disbelief transition to anger and frustration. Tearstained faces and others with clenched jaws stared at one another as we began to accept the struggle our church family was about to endure. The unimaginable was happening. Our pastor had violated his marriage vows and betrayed his congregation.

Our family was falling apart.

I gave the first public interview to a local Denver news station while walking out of the World Prayer Center at 11:15 p.m. It ran on national cable news stations all day long on Friday, but I never saw it. I was at the hospital!

The conflicting emotions in my heart seemed to physically affect my whole body. If the eyes are the window to the soul, then those nurses and doctors saw a tempest inside of me. I felt overjoyed one moment and agonized the next. I was thrilled by the prospect of our newest arrival and yet full of turmoil and fear.

My wife was amazing! Since this was our fifth (and final) child, the doctor asked if I wanted to help deliver. It was a side of childbirth that I had never before witnessed. Usually, I was there as my wife's coach, helping her breathe with my futile attempts to push along with her, saying encouraging things from time to time, and trying to perceive when to shut up. It was hard work … not as hard as the work she was doing, but difficult nonetheless. There was danger involved as well: fingernail marks on my flesh, screams in my ear at close range, even a headlock during an extended push. I was happy to sit where the doctor usually sits to witness this miracle and receive this new little life into my hands.

After several pushes, the baby crowned, and the doctor started to say things like, "Wait, wait, don't push too hard yet," and, "This boy may be a little bigger than I thought." Finally, this wrinkly mass of joyous flesh and bone, blood and water, entered our world. I caught him with my own two hands and held him in my arms, Dad and baby both crying in this moment of miracle and mess, wonder and wailing.

Aimee leaned back feeling the relief that follows God's great birthing process. I cut the umbilical cord, and we laid my son on the scale. I can still remember the surprised "oohs" and "ahhs" in the room as the numbers came up on that little digital screen: 10.05 pounds.

One family was growing, birthing, and celebrating. The other family was wounded, disillusioned, and bewildered. One family was staring into the future with bright-eyed wonder and anticipation. The other family wrestled with the past, and felt fearful of what the future would hold. I was part of both families.

These are the experiences, the moments, and the challenges that make us a family.

THE STRENGTH OF FAMILY

Families are amazingly resilient. Aimee and I did not plan to have five kids. She wanted three; I wanted four; so we had five. Neither of us are very good at math. It was the biggest surprise of our lives up to that point. Aimee cried for three weeks when we found out she was pregnant nine months earlier. But we pulled ourselves together and began the slow and steady process of preparing for a new season for our family—a season of feeling overwhelmed and overstressed, but a season of uncommon grace that would also fill our home with peace, joy, and contentment.

My church family would be no different. We were heading into a season of questions, trials, and grief, but we would also experience uncommon grace filling us with that same peace, joy, and contentment. This process was full of angst and anger. We all experienced deep frustrations and major freak-out moments, and of course, the bonds of our family were tested.

But I've never seen a family of believers come together like New Life Church did in the months and years after that day. We did what families always do when hard times hit. We pulled together. We cried together and consoled each other. We stayed together and loved each other into the healing and grace that God gave us in that season. We began to understand our identity as a family.

We began to see that we were more than just a group of people who were called New Lifers. We were something more. Through this wilderness of failure and faith, we learned that we weren't just a religious corporation, a rowdy pep rally for God, or even an organization that helps the poor, as good as that is. We weren't a manufacturer of curriculum to boost self-esteem, or a program for people who can't figure life out. What we learned in our most difficult season at New Life Church was that we were a *family*—good, bad, ugly, beautiful, weak, strong, foolish, and fiery … a true family.

As a member of a large family, I can assure you that families don't come in neat and tidy shrink-wrapped packages. Families aren't revealed through picture-perfect framed glass. For many, the idea of "family" doesn't evoke warm feelings of Norman Rockwell–like paintings of inviting fireplace gatherings and dinner-table prayers. Families are filled with grit and grime, sunshine and storms, whining as well as wonder. Families contain stories of tragedy and triumph, fun and foolishness, grace as well as gunk—*or grace in the midst of gunk.*

The family is where we're supposed to learn how to love deeply, fight fairly, share justly, work willingly, and survive during tough times. In families we are given our best opportunity to discover the basic building blocks of identity, history, heritage, meaning, and purpose. In a family we learn how to work hard, sort out injustice with siblings, and wrestle through disappointment with our parents. We learn expressions of love, humor, manners, and humility, all within the family context.

The family analogy is the best picture of what a healthy and vibrant church community is supposed to look like. If you think about it, families are perfectly designed for discipleship: constant access, consistent modeling, demonstration, teaching and training, conflict management and resolution, failure, follow-up and feedback. And this should all happen in an attitude and atmosphere of love. Children are raised, parents are matured, and grandparents are valued all at the same time.

This is God's design.

But our churches don't tend to have the characteristics of families anymore. Instead, we are more often full of consumers looking for our next God product, bingeing and purging Sunday to Sunday with a steady diet of fast-food TV preachers. We don't often learn how to fight fair with loving correction and guidance but instead appear to be recruiting culture warriors to fight against an unholy society—or worse, against a perceived political opponent. We all hate religion but love our spiritual individualism with such passion that we may be creating a generation of dechurched orphans who have no authentic spiritual family or heritage.

We're losing our children and teenagers. Our college students are disappearing from our pews. Demographic niches and consumer conveniences are not attracting the next generation to join us. The longevity of a church community is not even considered in the model of church that appeals to just one particular segment of society. We might be rearranging deck chairs on the *Titanic*.

The big *C* Church is on the verge of a massive shift philosophically and generationally. We are addicted to instant gratification. Microwave Christianity has replaced cooking the family meal. Instead of filming a movie classic, we're capturing YouTube videos. Instead of taking long, leisurely walks, we're making mad dashes to the mall. Instead of saving for our children's inheritance, we're buying lottery tickets. Our picture of who we are as the church is woefully inadequate and tragically shortsighted.

We are not learning enough from each other. We are not connecting generationally, and we are not birthing new family members. Most tragically, we are not making enough disciples to make a dent in our current culture. We're sneezing into the wind.

EXTREME HOME MAKEOVER

The idea of *church* is undergoing a massive makeover in America today. We desperately need a new paradigm for doing ministry so we can create the kind of community and connection that our culture longs for and needs. With skyrocketing divorce rates and family dysfunction in America at an all-time high, no wonder our churches are experiencing their own tragic crisis of definition and purpose. The argument raging over attractional church or missional church is valuable for us but may not be the whole story. We've seen purpose-driven, power-driven, culture-driven, and seeker-driven movements evolve, and while they all have something very good to say about how church should be done, we may have missed this fundamental and foundational principle that shapes who the church is: the fact that we are the family of God.

The Scriptures are full of this imagery. Family is the picture we get from the very beginning when Adam and Eve lived in the garden in Genesis 1. God saves one family in the story of Noah and the ark. God chooses the family line of Abraham, Isaac, and Jacob to be a blessing to the nations in Genesis 12, and the story continues as Esau and Jacob fight it out over birthrights, property, and livestock. The twelve tribes of Israel are the family lines of Jacob's twelve sons, who learn the lessons of God's sovereignty in the sibling rivalry of the story of Joseph. Moses, his brother, Aaron, and sister, Miriam, are all part of the story of leading the deliverance of God's people out of Egypt.

The good news for us is that each of these families is deeply flawed. Violence, forgiveness, betrayal, trust, and loyalty all play out in the drama of God's great story. This should encourage us as we read the Bible because we can see ourselves in it. These family stories present a vivid and beautiful picture of God interacting with imperfect and messy humanity. God is not interested in His people reflecting some kind of unattainable perfection. But He does want us to learn how to be healthy, secure, and sure of our calling as we embrace one another in honesty, love, truth, and grace. He's teaching us about family.

In the New Testament, the apostle Paul described the church as a "household of faith" (Gal. 6:10 ESV). He called Timothy his true son in the faith, and he coached and encouraged him not to give up and to be strong. Paul addressed his letters to the churches in each city as his brothers and sisters. He told the church at Corinth they had many guardians but not many fathers as he made his case for a parental relationship with them. Jesus even chose two sets of brothers to follow Him as disciples and described those who did God's will as His "mother, sisters, and brothers" (see Mark 3:35). Jesus taught His disciples that prayer is not just addressing God as Yahweh, but as our heavenly Father.

The Bible is a family book. It is a story about family—God's family.

REFRIGERATOR PRIVILEGES

Our Sunday mornings at church ought to have the kind of feeling that we have when we invite people over to our house. Of course, we clean it up a little more than normal because we don't want people to see how we really live—at least not at first—too embarrassing. But then as we get comfortable with them, we find that we really can let them in. As the relationship grows, they get to see how we really live.

They have refrigerator privileges.

You know, the kind of relationships you have with family members and friends who can come over and look in your refrigerator

for something to eat at any time of the day or night. That's exactly
how church should be! We need the kind of family that knows us,
our fears and faults, but loves us anyway; the kind of family that will
invest and forgive no matter what. It's a community of people who
share privileges and responsibilities as we learn how to live together
in harmony. Church can't be a place where we feel like a visitor, or
somewhere we're afraid to allow others to see our messes. It's got to
feel like home.

Most of us have grown up thinking churches are not messy
places. They are clean, tidy, orderly. We spend our Sunday mornings fixing our hair, applying the right amount of makeup, ironing
our shirts, and straightening our ties. At home we may fight about
breakfast, get angry at our spouse for being late—causing us to settle
for a bad parking spot—and finally threaten our kids with no TV or
candy if they whine about going to church.

But when we walk through the church doors, everything
changes. We put on our best Sunday smiles. We swap stories about
how wonderful life is going. We laugh, we shake hands during the
time when we're supposed to greet the people near us, and we smile
and nod along with the sermon. We don't want everyone there to
know the truth. We have problems. Sometimes frightening, overwhelming problems. Our homes are on the brink of foreclosure; our
marriages are crumbling and on the edge of divorce; our children are
getting bullied and being pressured into doing the unthinkable.

We don't like to bring our messy lives into the church. We're
scared that it will unsettle the pews. We don't want to feel out of
place, unaccepted, and unwelcome at the potluck. We don't want
people to judge our mess.

So we keep smiling.

We keep acting like things are okay.

We take our messes home where they belong.

We've viewed our churches like health clubs instead of hospitals. We've treated one another like convenient consumers instead of real families. But in a family there is no hiding the messiness. Everyone knows what's going on in our life, and it can make us feel awkward and vulnerable. Acceptance and love are part of the raw and gritty realness of family. Openness and honesty are what's required if the church is to be viable for the next generation. And make no mistake, they are watching, listening, and hoping for the kind of vulnerability and acceptance that will challenge them to be part of an imperfect yet loving church family.

My son Owen Alexander was born at 9:32 a.m. on November 3, 2006. He represents the next generation to me, and I want him to grow up in a world where the church in America is not hyped up on consumer-driven experiences and perfectly designed, robotic, or predictable worship services. I don't want him to experience church as overly simplistic answers and polished PowerPoint presentations. I want him to experience a real flesh-and-blood church, full of the strength that comes from Christ in the middle of our weakness. I want him to have the opportunity to see Christ in a community of people where love is the driving force and where sacrifice is more than mere lip service.

I want Owen to enjoy a real, honest, and authentic church family.

Chapter 2

CHURCH SHOPPING

GOD FOR SALE?

Searching for a church can be one of the most difficult experiences a Christian can have. You pull into the parking lot and take a deep breath. It's time to pump up the family before you get out of the car. "This could be it!" you say, with enthusiasm. You hope it is.

Walking through the doors, you pass friendly faces that greet you as sweetly as Walmart employees. They all seem familiar, but you don't recognize anyone. As you follow the signs telling you where to drop off the kids, you're all smiles, but then you notice that look in your child's eyes that makes you feel as if you're somehow abandoning her.

You wander into the main auditorium to find a seat and immediately begin to scan the room. You're looking for connection, for some sign that you belong. *Do they have a coffee bar?* you think to yourself. *Maybe a caramel macchiato will help.*

The worship service begins, but it's a challenge because you're keeping your eyes open while everyone else's eyes are closed, wondering if your child's number will show up on the screen. The offering plate goes by. You listen to the sermon with the critical ear of a seminary theologian. The pastor prays. You pick up the kids after service—"How was your class today?" Finally, in the car, you glance at your husband or your wife as you're exiting the parking lot. You both know it. You just feel it. This isn't it.

It's unavoidable when people move to a new area or when a church changes pastors, but looking for a new church happens often enough in other less-benevolent circumstances that American Christians everywhere know the experience.

As the complexity of the modern worshipper increases, shopping for a church has become the stuff of marketing experts and graphic designers. Every church, including ours, is doing its best to make guests feel warm and welcome, and who can fault us for that? Isn't that what we're supposed to be doing? The simple answer is yes. But somewhere between the "Holy Grounds" coffee bar and the aromatherapy candles, we may have gotten off course.

Church shopping is not really the problem, but this practice reveals so much about the problem. The pathway to finding a new church is littered with snares because it makes you the reviewer, the critic, the secret shopper! You look at everything through more critical eyes. You don't want to admit it, but you actually end up like the young, single college student making a list of qualities for the perfect, unblemished spouse of his or her future.

The problem? There are no perfect spouses.

I don't have anything against lists, and I'm all for people seeking a church family, but I wonder if we've created a monster.

The unique twenty-first-century experience of "church shopping" eluded me. I am the son of a Pentecostal pastor, and therefore have never had a choice in the matter. My parents raised me in the church's front row. If the doors were open, we were in church. As a pastor of small churches during my growing-up years, my dad did everything from preaching to plumbing. Mom played the piano and organ, while my brothers and I sang "specials" and taught Sunday school. I received glaring looks from Mom during worship more than once after forgetting to change transparencies on the overhead projector.

Churches are a lot like families. There are kids and cousins, parents and grandparents, teenagers and college students. And, of course, every family has a weird uncle Harold. I guess that's why church shopping or trying out worship services week after week can be so awkward. Let's face it: no one gets to choose his or her own family. You are born into them. Even adopted children don't choose their parents, they get chosen, and so it would seem that trying to choose your own church would have the same difficulties. I mean, you know your own family. Would you choose them? How does anyone intentionally choose to make weird uncle Harold a part of his or her family?

I believe becoming part of a church family is a lot more like realizing you've come home and less like going down a checklist or joining an organization. In fact, it's probably much more of a spiritual birthing process than we'd like to admit. We're born into the family of God, and I think it's accurate to say that we're born into a church family as well. Hopefully these things happen at the same time, and our church expands by conversion growth instead of transfer growth from other churches. However, many Christians have had that feeling of connectedness to a family of believers even knowing that this church is not the kind of church they would have chosen on their own. For some reason, they just "feel" like they've come home.

I remember attending the spring program at my daughter Grace's elementary school. It was so sweet to watch the kids sing their songs and share their poetry. Grace looked extremely cute in her new dress. The boy right in front of her sang loudly and off key the whole time. One kid on the end of the row picked his nose for much of the program. The teacher wasn't a good speaker and the sound system was poor. We sat in a gymnasium on bleachers, but every parent seemed to enjoy the program. In fact, they thought this program was so important that they all filmed it with their digital cameras! Along with all the other parents, I recorded each moment, listening, smiling, and laughing. It wasn't a smooth program, but I didn't care. Gracie is mine and I enjoyed her! Aimee and I enjoyed the program not because of what we got out of it but because my little girl, part of our family, participated. I wasn't so much a critic as I was a supportive and loving family member. Similarly, the acknowledgment of our roles as family members plays a big part in how we view church. Cosmetics and style are no substitute for an authentic family. People don't care if it's fancy or perfectly put together unless it's not a family. If you're joining a social club with status and reputation, then style points matter. But it's incredible to be part of a church where you know you belong and you know it's not perfect, but it's your family.

CONSUMERS OR FAMILY MEMBERS?

If we're not careful, we can easily fall into the trap of becoming consumers of goods and services rather than the family members God designed us to be. The apostles Paul and Peter both referred to the first-century believers as a family, and this description is especially meaningful and necessary in our modern-day application of church. If we don't understand this, it's easy for us to slide into thinking about the song selection, evaluating the sermon, or wondering why the pastor didn't say hi to us in the lobby. The truth is, we are part of something greater than our own personal preferences or felt needs. We are part of a worldwide family of believers who belong to each other with a history and a heritage defined by a loving heavenly Father.

There's nothing wrong with personal preferences or felt needs, and we certainly can't act as if our twenty-first-century American church culture doesn't exist. However, at the fundamental level, aren't we all searching for a family—a place to belong, to be fully known, and to be accepted for who we are? A place where our strengths are embraced and our weaknesses aren't swept under the proverbial rug?

Now, I'm not just a sentimental sap who thinks that everybody should settle for their church no matter how poor the preaching or how out of tune the worship. I'm a fan of honest evaluations for the sake of our churches serving people more effectively. I want our churches to reinvent themselves and make the message more accessible and appealing, mobilizing every one of us to carry this message into our own "world." But in the American church culture, we've all swallowed the Kool-Aid and become professional critics.

The whole thing just smacks of *American Idol.* (With my best announcer voice) "Can this church measure up to your expectations? Who will be your *next church family?*"

In our approach to church, we would never admit to being like Simon of *American Idol* and *The X Factor,* at least publicly, because he's so cynical. And most of the time he's just downright rude! But we all tend to think like him because he actually speaks the truth! Most of us are probably more like Paula Abdul in our responses—we say nice things about the cosmetics of a service and avoid any substantive analysis about our church. Either way, overemphasizing our evaluations of Sunday-morning performances just plain feels wrong.

But when you evaluate a church from a family perspective, it changes the way you analyze everything. Love becomes the motivation that guides your critique. You approach the process from a completely different paradigm. You think about what you can add to this family rather than what it can do for you. In fact, you are more willing to say hard things because you love this family and belong to it.

When you size up a church as a consumer and base your assessment on what that church can offer you, it creates an unhealthy frame of reference. This consumer paradigm forces us to conduct an analysis of the benefits, while the family paradigm fosters a sense of belonging. One paradigm is focused on you, and the other paradigm is focused on others.

Healthy families protect one another and give each other grace. Consumers investigate and scrutinize and determine whether or not they will purchase the services being provided. No doubt about it, families fight! But in the end, after all the tears and slammed doors, the family remains. However, consumers always keep their options open. Families share chores and responsibilities, while consumers believe they are owed something, especially if they have given money to the cause. A church service is not a business transaction between parties, but instead a loving exchange of service and worship. It doesn't always seem that simple, but foundationally, when we remove all the trappings, this familial attitude must remain.

The church is first and foremost a spiritual family and not a corporation or a nonprofit organization. Church structure, bylaws, and positions of authority are all necessary to an organization. But we should see these necessary elements through the lens of the family so that we don't get confused about who we are.

I have seen church planters try to manufacture a church culture by creating all the structure without first establishing the life of the church. They tend to focus on logistics at the expense of people, because dealing with business cards, leases, and websites is cleaner and easier. Recently, someone said to me, "It's a lot easier to add structure to life than it is to add life to structure." This gets to the heart of the matter: our spiritual life as a family of believers is the priority because it creates the genuine and authentic church. These family members can meet together whatever their 501(c)(3) status. We can meet in coffee shops and movie theaters, storefronts and old grocery stores, under a tree or in a cave. We can worship and serve one another even if tyrannical governments say we can't exist. We can meet in undisclosed locations under persecution and find ways to pray and share even when it means being disowned by our physical families. This family of believers is the church of Jesus Christ, and it takes precedence over all other man-made structures or authorities. In our twenty-first-century American church culture, we sometimes forget this essential and foundational truth.

HOW DID WE GET HERE?

In my experience, there are two primary sources for this tendency toward an ultracritical analysis of church in American culture. One is the seeker-church model, which has been with us for many years now. This model of church ministry has been a blessing to many American churches because it has emphasized the same principles the apostle

Paul taught in 1 Corinthians 12–14: essentially, the seeker model recognizes that people who haven't been to church before will be in our meetings. Make sure they can understand what God wants to say to them. Don't use language that unchurched people cannot recognize. Put some energy and creativity into crafting transformational moments for believers and unbelievers alike. This is an evangelistic model that finds other avenues besides Sunday morning for believers to gather. But this model has also fueled an overemphasis on the tendency toward "church as theater," as well as an obsession with perfectly programmed church services.

Frankly, I'm not sure we need perfectly orchestrated services. We certainly need to clean up and welcome guests just like a family that has invited others over for dinner. We don't need to show our guests all of our dirty laundry and "junk drawers" on their first visit. That would just be silly. But neither do we need to create the quintessential environment of seeming perfection and niceness. Families aren't nice; trust me, I'm in one!

What I mean is that there are many other emotions, conflicts, and experiences that are valuable and useful to a family. Some churches are so committed to eliminating every single distraction or discomfort that they've created a sterile, placid portrait of a family as opposed to an actual family. And in our society, the next generation is wary of anything too produced and organized. They want it to be raw and real. They can see right through anything fake.

The second source of this church critique is newer on the cultural landscape of Christianity in America. About fifteen years ago we all began experiencing the effects of the "postmodern" philosophical movement that challenged many of our views of church. The trend has been to question everything, and the questioning itself, for some, has become the answer. The desire to be relevant has all too often led to an approach that favors style over substance, an approach that most churches now are reexamining.

I'm not saying that this movement was empty and meaningless. On the contrary, our twenty-first-century American culture changed rapidly in the last fifteen years, and many churches were left behind intellectually and spiritually. We all struggled to understand how to relate to this new "experiential" model of ministry versus a more "intellectual" model, and the postmodern discussion helped us engage in the cultural dialogue about what, if anything, should happen within our churches.

There is no doubt both of these movements challenged us to find a more meaningful paradigm for what church should be in America. Both of these movements began to move the church outside of its walls and paved the way for the focus on the missional church talked about so much today. Instead of always looking in, we've started to look out, and that is a much healthier point of view. But we still must understand who we are as we go out into this world. The bottom line for me is we're all searching for a church culture that creates belonging, meaning, and purpose no matter what our religious background. We all want to create experiences that will give us the best opportunity to reach people with the message of Jesus. However, we have to go far beyond just church-growth techniques or cultural relevance.

We're talking about more than just an environment.

We're describing a community.

We're longing for a family.

FAMILY DNA

I'm amazed at the rootless and orphan-like outlook of many who have shown up to ONEchapel in our urban setting of Austin, Texas. If you know anything about Austin, it has the reputation of being a hip culture influenced by the students of the University of Texas, lots of hippies who encourage the city's motto, "Keep Austin Weird," and the many musicians and artists who create an eclectic and independent vibe. There are families in our city, but there is also a disproportionately large single population that influences our city outlook.

These people all seem to be longing to belong.

There is a tendency for new churches like ours to appeal to this trendy postmodern environment with all of the laid-back attitudes and intellectual intensity that form the stereotypical "emerging" churches. But our approach has been almost countercultural. Not necessarily because we need to be different, but because we want to emphasize family. Psalm 68:6 says, "God sets the lonely in families." And we have seen the need in Austin for people to feel the love and acceptance of a family culture. They're starving for it.

Don't get me wrong. Our worship is strong and filled with God's presence; the Bible teaching is pretty good (if I do say so myself), and we have a strong mission focus—we saw over 250 people make decisions for Christ in our first year alone. But the sense of love, family, and acceptance is what people responded to most.

We are bound together by a clear message and a purpose. There is love in the room when we gather. There is an understanding that we're all growing together in different stages of life and faith, and the acceptance people feel is punctuated by the fact that so many from diverse backgrounds have joined this family. Our name emphasizes this idea that we are united as one, even though we come from various religious upbringings, political affiliations, and economic situations within different racial and cultural contexts.

Isn't this what the church is supposed to be about?

The last verse in the Old Testament holds a powerful truth and testimony of what God is trying to accomplish between the generations. The cry of Malachi 4:6 is to heal our families and see God's people united in obedience and love. Read slowly and take in the implications of this verse—the final words before the revelation of God's Son in the New Testament.

> He will turn the hearts of the parents to their chil-
> dren, and the hearts of the children to their parents;
> or else I will come and strike the land with total
> destruction.

The precursor to the total destruction of a society is families falling apart, turning against one another in violation, bitterness, disappointment, and anger. When the hearts of children come against their parents and the hearts of the parents are out of touch with their children, then the land is cursed.

The church of Jesus Christ can be the powerful example of a family that turns the fullness of their hearts toward one another generationally. This attitude is truly "countercultural" in opening the door to the gospel message—people birthed into the family of God. People outside the family want to be accepted. Orphans longing for love; old people craving a legacy. This is how it happens. Fathers and mothers turn their hearts toward their children, and the children reciprocate. It's a powerful vision and goal for the church.

THE GOD-GIVEN PRIMAL INSTINCT OF FAMILY

The power of true family connections is amazing, because people will do almost anything for their family. They may fight with one another, but when an outsider attacks someone in the family, they'll defend each other to the bitter end. The family bond is difficult to break.

I experienced this truth on a crisp winter day in December 2007. It was a Sunday morning, and I had led worship that day at New Life Church. The previous night had left a blanket of snow on the ground that had begun to melt away in the warm Colorado sun. We had a special guest speaker that day, the highly respected pastor Jack Hayford, former senior pastor of The Church On The Way in Van Nuys, California, and a pastor to pastors. That morning, Pastor Jack shared an amazing Christmas message with our New Life family.

After the service, I was invited to eat lunch with Pastor Jack by Brady Boyd (New Life's senior pastor), up in his office. Pastor Brady had been officially installed as the senior pastor of New Life Church just three months earlier, and he and I were starting to forge an authentic friendship. Also, I was excited to spend quality time with a man of Pastor Jack's respected stature within the body of Christ.

Lunch progressed at a leisurely pace over salad and sandwiches while we discussed the health of the church and future plans. Suddenly, a loud clatter at the door interrupted our friendly gathering. I'll never forget the looks on the faces of Pastor Daniel Grothe and Pastor Brady's administrative assistant, Karla Leathers, who burst through the door of Pastor Brady's office, red faced, as if they were trying to escape from some horrible monster.

They both said simultaneously, "We have shots fired in the building."

As they began to describe what they knew, I immediately bolted out of the room. I'm kind of embarrassed to say I didn't wait for instructions or a plan from Pastor Brady. I didn't wait for any words of wisdom from one of the most revered and intelligent men in the modern church, Pastor Jack.

I ran out the door, consumed by the thought of my thirteen-year-old son, Zachary, who was downstairs in the lobby where a lone gunman armed with a thousand rounds of ammunition was now shooting people.

The rest is a bit of a blur in my memory, but I recall running down the hallway of the second floor of New Life Church toward the Children's Ministry area. I knew from the report that some people might have been shot, but I didn't know the details. I just knew that I had to go find my son.

It didn't matter what the cost was going to be to myself; I had to get to him and make sure he was safe. It was a primal, parental urge that didn't require thought or calculation. It was instinct. He was my family.

I could hear the shots being fired downstairs as I was running through the hallway, trying to figure out if I could get to him without getting shot. Questions raced through my head: Is my son okay? Is he being shot right now? How many of them are there? Did he get out of the building in time? Where is he right now?

I tried to call him on my cell phone. He didn't answer.

I decided to use the back staircase in the corner of our building—most people didn't even know it was there. It was right next to an exit.

My eyes could barely stand the afternoon sun as I pushed the door open and stumbled through the snow. I saw a few people running and confused. I heard the screams of a woman to my left somewhere in the parking lot as I walked low between cars. I finally got Zachary on the phone as I tried to figure out all that was happening. He couldn't explain where he was … behind a Dumpster somewhere. Our call was cut off. So many others were calling loved ones or calling 911. Cell service was jammed. The police started to arrive, yelling at people to get out of the parking lot.

Zachary called. I told him to head over to Pikes Peak Community College next to our property and get as far away from the building as possible. I couldn't find my car—my brain could not recall where I'd parked that morning several hours earlier. Finally, I found my Explorer and drove to the college to find Zachary and some friends I picked up and took home.

I can't explain the sense of relief I felt when I saw him. He's my oldest child, and I had never experienced the kind of concern I had over him that day. I learned something about myself in that experience: my love for him is worth any danger that I will ever face. I'm willing to risk my life, pay any price, and do just about anything to rescue him. I love him deeply, and that drives me in the midst of a crisis.

I would gladly trade my life for his.

This story reminds me of God's love for us. We are long-lost prodigal sons and daughters, and He longs for us to come home. He sent Jesus to find us, speak to us, and show us the way back to Him. He's our heavenly Father, and He loves us so much that He gave His only Son that whoever would believe in Him would have eternal life (John 3:16). He was willing to risk sending His own Son to die so that we could live.

I also immediately think about David and Marie Works, who lost two daughters that day. The lone gunman shot them outside in our church parking lot, and David was wounded badly. Before the gunman could fire at any others, a security guard mortally wounded Matthew Murray inside the building in a heroic, aggressive act. I most likely heard her gunshots as I was running down the stairs.

It had been a terrifying day for me, but nothing compared to what David and Marie faced. Their daughters, Rachel and Stephanie, were teenagers who loved Jesus and whose lives were tragically cut short. It's hard to imagine the pain and grief that David and Marie endured. Our church grieved with them and became another extended family for them.

I'll always remember how they showed up every Sunday morning as the months of grief unfolded. I would look out into the congregation and see them to my left as I led worship from the stage at New Life Church. Their strength speaks to all of us. But the loss still stings. Family bonds are strong.

Their story is remarkably told in their book, *Gone in a Heartbeat*, as well as Pastor Brady Boyd's book *Fear No Evil*.

This event communicates how valuable family is to all of us. It reveals how the idea of family is hardwired into us as humans. God designed it that way. This is how it is supposed to be. He describes us throughout the Scriptures as His children. He is our Father, and we are all brothers and sisters who love Him. We are the family of God. It is a paradigm-changing concept that needs to be embraced by the church of today, but it's even more necessary when held up against the consumer concept of our twenty-first-century American church model. When we compare the two, the consumer approach reveals a self-centered and individualistic mind-set. It appeals to the worst of our human nature instead of challenging us to live outside of ourselves. It is flimsy, weak, and foolish compared to the stability, power, and wisdom of a family of believers.

Our churches can be so much more.

Our love for one another can communicate so much more.

Our family bond can be strong.

If only we will come to the table together.

Chapter 3

EATING ALONE AT CHURCH

DINNER, DIVORCE, AND DISRUPTION

Have you ever noticed how kids don't want to sit down at the dinner table? They squirm and wiggle as if there were ants in their pants. They kneel on their chairs, hang one cheek off the seat, flip and twirl throughout dinner.

Ethan is our current wiggly worm. He twists and turns around in his chair. He stands up, wanders off from time to time, picks at his food, and complains that his throat hurts. He fights with his brother who sits beside him, and is generally uninterested in anything remotely resembling food.

About every two weeks we'll be having dinner and talking, and suddenly Ethan will completely disappear from the table with a huge thud. Ethan falls out of his chair and hits the floor. He loses whatever food was on his fork for the last ten minutes or slaps his plate on the way down, tossing beans and potatoes into the air. Then he cries— *loudly*. He's embarrassed, and that makes him mad at everyone else at the table who is now laughing at him. We comfort him and tell him to sit on his chair with his feet in front. "You have to eat five more beans before you are excused," his mother typically tells him.

It's at moments just like this when Aimee and I realize how much we appreciate date nights. The dinner table is a wonderful and

meaningful component of our family fabric, but my wife is so grateful for grown-up conversation at a dinner where she doesn't have to
eat quickly and feed two or three others at the same time. In other
words, our family dinners typically involve hard work. Dinner out
with couples is a wonderful treat. Come to think of it, I don't know
if I've ever seen my wife eat at our dinner table. She's always serving
and feeding and helping us—the family.

The family dinner table has a very different atmosphere from
when my wife and I go out and join two couples for dinner. One
is full of adult conversation and pleasantries where one can actually tell a story all the way through without being interrupted by
screaming, spilling, or crying. The other is an atmosphere of crying,
laughing, loud talking, banging, complaining, threatening, singing,
and whistling.

It's even more adventurous when our extended family is at our
dinner table. Picture the scene. Grandma and Grandpa, aunts and
uncles, cousins, and in-laws gather to enjoy dinner together. There is
something significant about the sense of community and excitement
that pervades the atmosphere when we come together.

Thanksgiving, Christmas, birthdays, and graduations are all
special days for the whole family to be together. It is incredible to
me how my grandmother and my mom used to slave over the turkey,
dressing, sweet potato pie, and green bean casserole, only to have the
entire family ingest an insane amount of food in the span of about
fifteen minutes.

Of course, we always made enough for leftovers, and I love the
atmosphere that the second round of gluttonous eating creates. People
would sit and talk and eat and talk and eat some more—usually for

several hours—we'd watch a little football and then get up and do it all over again. This is an environment full of stories, memories, and laughter, which become memories in and of themselves.

What's the first thing you notice when the whole family gets together during these holidays? Arguing, right? Okay, but there is something besides the awkward discussions about politics, the snippy comments about family history, or even the crazy stories from your tipsy uncle Harold. If you reflect on family holidays and gatherings, you will recall something so meaningful and so profound that it can come only through a family.

You might see older adults helping the young children get their food. You'll notice teenagers bearing with their grandparents' special needs by serving them and listening to long stories of what it was like when they were kids—flapping dentures and all. Middle-age parents coax their teenagers into conversations, and it seems that everyone is willing to hold the babies—that is until the baby has a special gift for an unsuspecting family member.

The difference between a nice calm meal out with adults and the family gathering at the dinner table is quite striking. One is easy, the other difficult. One is self-directed while the other is focused on others. One is individualistic and the other is communal. One has nice moments of conversation and the other a roar of activity, mess, and work. Both are good, and both are necessary to create healthy families.

The family eating and sharing together forces everyone to acknowledge that others are at the table. We look around the table and see each generation represented, and we are forced to really "see" them, to genuinely hear them, and to ultimately know and understand them. Unfortunately, these bigger gatherings usually happen only once or twice a year for too many families.

There is a beautiful and important truth discovered when the whole family comes to the table. It's a virtue that makes these gatherings enjoyable even though they are accompanied by a tremendous amount of effort. This ethic of family values may seem obvious, but much of our niche-marketed, individualized culture has lost sight of it.

DIVORCE CULTURE

The traditional family is becoming a foreign concept for much of our society. The family is undergoing a seismic shift in definition and practice as we continue our social and cultural experimentation with what a family should be in America. Consider the sad truth that the majority of Americans experience their holidays through the filter of their own broken families. These days, statistically more than 50 percent of our families must figure out how to split time between stepparents, half brothers, and half sisters. The pain of divorce is felt at every Christmas, Thanksgiving, graduation, wedding, and special family event. The discomfort and injustice of broken families inevitably taint the festivities, but worse, they mark the hearts of each family member with a scar of distrust, pain, and loss.

I know this pain firsthand.

I was raised in a pastor's home—born on Saturday and in church on Sunday, if you know what I mean. I lived a pretty charmed life in an average, middle-class family where my dad served small churches of two hundred or fewer people. Life was innocent until the age of seventeen when everything that I knew as solid and foundational began to crumble around me. My parents' marriage fell apart. No immorality or physical abuse, just poor communication and a slow slipping away of the priorities of the family. Ministry became all-consuming, and my parents' relationship eroded without anyone noticing, least of all, my two younger brothers and me. They were good parents but flawed in their ability to connect to each other. In a season of pressure and difficulty their flaws became frustrations, their frustrations became failures, and finally, their failures fractured the relationship.

I remember feeling the ache in the pit of my stomach at every meal as our family fell apart. I felt the same way at every church service where deacons began to side with one of my parents. Everything I thought of as foundational and steady became a tornado of destruction in my church and in my family. Elders fought, Mom and Dad squared off, board members threatened, people left our church, and a deafening silence hovered over the dinner table with my brothers and father.

These are still incredibly painful memories. But there are two miracles that rose from the ashes of my own heartache and perseverance. The first miracle was the fact that God met me in the midst of my young struggle to find my own faith. I found Him for myself in the most tangible and meaningful way during that year of weakness and pain.

The second miracle is that both of my brothers and I are in full-time local church ministry. Somehow God protected us from the wounds and cynicism that typically occur in a story like ours. We all ministered together for several years in the same church, and we're each committed to loving, healthy marriages (our first and only marriages).

The truth is that all three of us should have a deep mistrust of "church people." After our experience, we should believe that the church is full of hypocrites and hidden agendas. I know these types of people do attend our churches, but God has given us grace and insight into the way humanity is made, and He has turned it all around in our lives for His purposes. We love the local church and the family that it represents.

Lastly, in seventeen years of local church ministry, I have seen countless marriages saved as a result of my story. I've been able to confidently and lovingly pastor many struggling couples through dysfunction, estrangement, and even adultery. I've seen marriages healed, put back together, and pulled back from the brink of destruction because of my own personal story. My experience in walking through the difficulty of divorce and the pain of a broken family, as well as the challenges of a blended family, has given me greater understanding. I'm thankful that God took what could have been so destructive in my life and changed it into something useful in His hands. Our family has been healed of the hurts. My dad has remarried, and that blended family has been a blessing. My relationship with both of my parents is healthy and whole, and we all have experienced the love of our heavenly Father putting us back together.

I'm thankful for the miracles that God grants to heal hearts and to mend broken families, but this divorce culture has changed the way American Christians look at our church family. We fear commitment. It is difficult for us to open our hearts in a church when those hearts have gaping wounds created by those closest to us. We are uncomfortable with conflict. In fact, we have embraced a theology that releases us from any conflict. It is a misinterpretation of

Matthew 7:1: "Judge not, that ye be not judged" (KJV). American individualism has overtaken our understanding of a biblical community and causes us to ask, "What right do we have to impose our views on someone else?" Somewhere between our desires to fit in with our culture and not be perceived as judgmental and our fear of conflict, we choose to "live and let live."

Matthew 7 is an encouragement to evaluate yourself *before* you try to evaluate others. Jesus actually said it this way in verse 5: "You hypocrite, first take the plank out of your own eye, and then you will see clearly to remove the speck from your brother's eye." Notice that Jesus didn't tell us to stop removing the speck from our brother's eye; He just said it is a lot easier to see once the plank is out of our own eye.

Our families are God's first classroom in life for learning about selfishness and love, fighting and sharing, disappointment and justice. This is one of the purposes of family: to learn how to fight fair, to share what we have, and to root selfishness out of our lives.

I can tell you this. I have five children, and I didn't have to teach one of them how to be selfish. I didn't have to teach them how to take what they want. They do it very naturally. What I do have to teach them is that they must share and care for people in order to live successfully with others. They have to learn how to argue in a way that does not insult, violate, or abuse, but rather communicates what they believe and what they need.

Fighting is part of life. I heard somebody say one time, "Where two or three are gathered, there will be a difference of opinion." It is true. We can't live together with our family, our church, our neighbors, or our community without some arguments, fights, or disagreements. Learning how to navigate those relationships successfully and validating the opinions of others is how we settle disputes. The success of our lives depends upon how we give, receive, and process feedback. If we don't do this well, we become isolated and self-absorbed.

We all must learn how to fight, forgive, and forget. The signs of a healthy family are these: they understand how to fight fair, they forgive easily, and they forget the past willingly without holding a grudge. All families fight. But some families fight to the death.

When a family fights in a divorce culture, the great fear is that someone might leave. The culture of divorce has had a profound effect on our society and in the way that we process conflict. The impact on our church communities has been no less revealing—many of our churches are quite dysfunctional. If our own families don't know how to get along, is it any wonder that our church families don't know how to share with one another or process the conflict that will inevitably rise to the surface?

The truth is most of us end up preferring isolation in our church. It's safer and there's no risk of getting hurt. I've got my relationship with Jesus and you've got yours. If I need some help, I'll open up—*a little*—maybe, and receive the initial benefits of community, but as for laying my heart out there to a group of people who may leave or abuse it, that's not going to happen.

This is the true challenge for our church families, all of which live in a divorce culture.

DINNER TABLE

It wasn't long ago that dinner with the family meant something foundational to our society. The family dinner table was once an icon for that bedrock of safety and security that comes from consistent communion, training, discussion, and sharing.

The dinner table is the place where the family has historically connected, where the family is defined and refined, and where each person finds his or her role and significance in the most basic building block of our social fabric. If you look at a family, it may have its hang-ups and idiosyncrasies, but if a family has dinner together on a consistent basis, there's a pretty good chance that it's relatively healthy.

My family has many schedule challenges! I have worked some long hours during the planting season of our new church, ONEchapel. We have five kids and a whirlwind of activities. Zachary is a now a junior in high school with his driver's license; Taylor is a freshman who loves singing; Grace is in sixth grade and playing volleyball, while Ethan is loving the social dynamics of first grade. Owen just turned five years old and goes to preschool three days a week. We have basketball, school functions, church services, gymnastics, music lessons, and we'd like to be able to enjoy our friends and their families too once in awhile.

Dinner has the potential to become our sacred time. It should be the gathering place after the family has enjoyed all of their separate activities throughout the day. Frankly, I think my wife would go crazy if she had to spend every minute of every day with the whole family together. And I personally like going to work and coming home at the end of the day. I think each member of the family should learn how to function as an individual, but what defines him or her, what provides identity, and what helps make each of them an outstanding individual are the love and connection to the family.

Dinnertime should be when we can tell the stories of our day, share our frustrations, laugh at our mistakes, and enjoy one another. But the Parsley family dinners bear no resemblance to the Norman Rockwell paintings of Americana.

THE PARSLEY CIRCUS (DINNERTIME)

Our family dinners are quite a spectacle, and if you have even one child in your family, you know what I mean. As more kids are added to the family, dinners get more exciting and more revealing as to what kind of family is actually gathered at the table.

As I mentioned earlier, I have five kids. Zachary and Taylor are my two oldest boys, seventeen and fifteen, respectively. They should both be experts in video games considering the amount of time they seem to devote to them. Gracie is my little princess, and at twelve years old she has become our resident artiste with her special talent for drawing hearts and horses. Ethan is seven years old and the most vocal of any of our children. He wants to talk every waking moment of every day and sometimes while he's sleeping. Owen is our sweet surprise baby, who is now just five years old. He's just getting over separation anxiety, which made his every outing a major emotional event.

It's like a giant circus everywhere we go. We walk into a restaurant and everyone stares. I can only guess what they're saying: "How do they afford to eat out?" "What a crazy life that must be!" "Somebody ought to tell them what's causing that!" I can feel their eyes making us the center of attention in the room.

Now, first-time parents are usually concerned about whether or not they'll be able to adequately care for their child. I know my wife was afraid that she wouldn't be able to keep Zachary alive after we brought him home from the hospital. With our secondborn, we felt as though we were starting to get the hang of this strange adventure called parenting. Our thirdborn was accompanied by an "I've got this, no problem!" And by the time the fourthborn came around, our response was, "Did you hear something?"

DISRUPTIVE FORCE

Every family in our American culture faces these kinds of challenges to protect their family in the midst of overwhelming options and opportunities. This is often the family's problem when prioritizing dinner. We are consumed by all of the possibilities! We have so many interests! Not only does each member of the family have multiple areas of interest, but we often participate in our interests individually instead of sharing experiences with one another.

It is tempting to have dinner individually, on different schedules, by placing one or two kids in front of the television, allowing another to play video games while Mom reads a magazine and Dad is catching up on work that must be done before tomorrow. As a result, this family cultivates being apart and, ultimately, becomes more individualistic and shallower in the deprioritization of the family.

We end up eating alone. Consuming what we need without the benefit and joy of sharing with loved ones. We become isolated in our TV show, newspaper, Facebook, Twitter, actual book, or video game, eating by ourselves without the acknowledgment of others or the training, selflessness, and understanding that can come only from dinner with others.

It's the mirror to the spiritual individualism that we practice in our culture. Everyone seems to be okay with God; we just don't like His family. So, we eat alone in our isolated spirituality, stuffing ourselves with the food of our own particular liking while our souls shrink, starving for the authentic communion of bread and wine in community. Really, what we're doing is placing our individual interests above our family interests. I'm reminded of Philippians 2, which challenges us to look to the interests of others and beyond our own. Eating alone is okay. It's not the greatest evil in the world, and we've all got to eat to live. But what are we missing when we choose to feed our hunger without the communion of sitting at a table with others?

Jesus Himself shows us the beauty of communion and the wonder of sharing a meal with others.

JESUS LOVED TO EAT WITH PEOPLE!

As we look at Jesus through the lens of the Gospels, we see a man who loved being with people. Not surprisingly, much of His ministry happened around food! That's a great combination: people and food! This pairing has the makings of a party, which Jesus seemed to find Himself in the middle of more than once. Think of it. The wedding in Cana, where He turned the water into wine; the multiplication of the loaves and the fish; the Last Supper; dinner with a Pharisee; Mary and Martha; Jesus, people, and food—it's everywhere in Scripture!

I can almost see Jesus in my city of Austin, Texas, hanging out down on South Congress Avenue, inviting people to eat with Him at Home Slice, my favorite pizza joint. He was the kind of guy who knew the power of fellowship, communion, and the breaking of bread together. And the best part was Jesus didn't care who you were—you were invited.

The Lord's Supper provides the most poignant imagery of how Jesus shared communion with others. Breaking bread with these twelve disciples shows us something that Jesus did that emphatically encourages the sharing of sacred meals between believers. Of course, this pattern was found first in the Old Testament during the Passover Feast, remembering and celebrating Israel's deliverance from Egypt. The Passover meal is an entire experience of its own with specific instructions about how to cook and prepare the food. The meal includes bitter herbs that remind one of slavery, leaving a portion for the Lord as an acknowledgment of His faithfulness, and sharing this meal together with friends and family—all of which were part of the backdrop, if you will, of Jesus's Last Supper.

What does this meal say about Jesus? First of all, I don't think He was a person who liked to eat alone. How else could you explain the miracle of the multiplication of the loaves and fish, not just on one occasion, but twice! Jesus loved eating with others and sharing what He had. Jesus valued eating with people! For Him it was a place to share values, to demonstrate acceptance, to challenge the status quo, and to communicate love. It might surprise you to realize that some of Jesus's greatest works came in the context of sharing a meal with others.

The religious leaders of His day called Jesus a "friend of sinners" because of His practice of eating with unsavory characters, social outcasts, and known sinners. One day Jesus actually invited Himself to dinner with a man named Zacchaeus, who was a corrupt tax collector sitting in a tree in order to see Jesus as He walked along with the crowd. The result of the dinner? Zacchaeus promised to pay back all that he had stolen from the people, plus more! That's quite a meal.

Jesus was willing to eat with all kinds, even Pharisees, who were constantly trying to undermine His ministry with their expertise. In Luke 7 Jesus allowed and encouraged a dinner interruption and a discussion about the needs of others when a sinful woman poured perfume on His feet and wiped them clean with her hair. Jesus was no stranger to crazy talks and inconvenient messes at dinner.

In fact, this is the whole point of dinner. Dinner allows for the distractions and discussions that cause us to share in genuinely open and vulnerable fellowship together. Jesus knew this and took advantage of it on many occasions.

Consider the preparation that was required for the Last Supper. Jesus sent His disciples to gather all of the necessary food and make arrangements with the owner of a house, and then they reclined at the table together just before He went to the cross. It was at this meal that Jesus both confronted Judas and challenged Peter. He invited them into His confidence and communion, but also challenged and corrected them in the same space. Jesus told us to practice this remembrance every time we share a meal.

All through the Gospels, Jesus told parables and stories about banquets, and He Himself is the centerpiece of the Marriage Supper of the Lamb. Jesus told people to eat His flesh and drink His blood. What did this mean? Seems a bit extreme. Might this be one of those moments where the eating analogy goes too far?

Not at all.

Jesus is communicating about hunger, satisfaction, life, and service. He wanted the disciples to lay down their lives like He was going to lay down His life. He wanted them to be filled with the life that only God could provide. Jesus called Himself the Bread of Life and the Bread that comes down from heaven. He used this metaphor to emphasize communion, sharing, and being satisfied with only Him!

Breaking bread was really just an extension of the relational ministry of Jesus. People were His focus and purpose. Sharing a meal is one of the best ways of engaging, interacting, and understanding.

The first-century Christians continued the practice described in Acts 2:42, which contains the original recipe of what I believe the church is supposed to be. It says, "They devoted themselves to the apostles' teaching and to fellowship, to the breaking of bread and to prayer." When we come together as a family at dinner, we are in good company, practicing the beauty of communion with one another as people have done since the very beginning of creation.

Have you ever noticed how vulnerable eating food in front of someone else can be? I know that many books have been written to help us all use proper etiquette and manners when we come to the table—which fork to use, elbows off the table, appropriate dinner topics, etc. But the truth is that eating with others opens us up somehow. We acknowledge a primal need in communion with each other. The walls come down a little bit, and we see each other more honestly.

I require two things at each of our ONEchapel Connect Groups: *food* and *prayer*. If they don't do anything else, at least they share sustenance and then pray for one another. Let's face it. It's truly humbling and revealing when we try to talk while eating. You just can't maintain all proper decorum when you're opening your mouth and putting food in it. Unless you're sitting at a really long table in an evening gown with expensive china and eight pieces of silverware and three glasses, eating food with others can really open you up.

Eating alone can be a self-absorbed and isolating experience. I am so social that I have a hard time seeing myself ever going to a restaurant and eating alone. I saw a sweet elderly woman eating alone this week, and the scene broke my heart. Now, I know she was probably fine with it, but I cannot stand the thought of eating all by myself. Surely this says more about me than it does about her, and certainly I have eaten alone before, but I don't like it!

I don't believe that being alone is the design God had in mind. He wants us consuming Him and sharing Him together. He wants us vulnerable with one another, sharing the intimate details of our hearts. God designed us to live in a community of selfless serving, sharing, and correction. The dinner table is one of the best analogies we can use to understand how the family of God might relate to one another. Jesus understood this design and loved to experience fellowship with others. We, as His family, must do the same. We must join one another at the table and, like so many families, look forward to the joy, the mess, the sharing, the training, the tastes, and the surprises of dinner together!

Chapter 4

THE FAMILY WORSHIP TABLE

The smell of fresh biscuits and crispy bacon wafted into the room, waking me from the kind of sound and peaceful sleep you can only get from lying on a feather bed in front of the oil stove in the living room at Grandma and Grandpa's house. We had traveled by car for two days to get to the magical and wonderful world of Cowiche, a tiny town with one stoplight and two train tracks just outside of Yakima, Washington.

For many years my grandparents Frank and Mabel Parsley lived across the street from the apple-packing plant in a two-bedroom house with no interior doors. Their house was a veritable wonderland of gardens and cornstalk rows, old tractor parts, trails, irrigation ditches, and a dirt floor garage, not to mention the huge oak tree in the front yard producing shade that often called for naps on beautiful summer afternoons. My brother Brad and I loved to go to Grandma's house. It was nothing like our house! And breakfast, well, let's get back to it.

Eggs, bacon, biscuits, gravy, sausage, and Trix cereal! We never got to eat sugary cereals at home, so this was a special treat! We would come to the table and eat until we were so full that we felt like we were going to pop. I loved eating with the whole family for breakfast—it was so comforting and connecting. I have warm memories of the aunts and uncles and cousins all gathering at Grandma and Grandpa's house for many a Thanksgiving meal or other special family events.

It seems to me that Sunday-morning church should feel a bit like this.

On Sunday mornings people should be as comfortable at church as they might be at Grandma's house. The dream is to create an environment where people come with anticipation and expectation of what God will say and do as we gather for worship. The family of God is about enjoying the bounty of God's table and fellowship with one another and with the Holy Spirit. I'm not just talking about greeters and graphics here. I'm talking about an atmosphere that people don't necessarily see but an environment that they can feel. Sunday church should be a welcoming family that comes to the table to worship together. I know, I know; most of you have used this moniker of *family* to describe your church, but relatively few churches actually do what's required to live together as a family.

"The family worship table" is a phrase that I began to use several years ago as I spoke at conferences and seminars on worship ministry. As a worship pastor for many years, I began to raise up a new generation of worship leaders at New Life Church in Colorado Springs, and our experience together began to form this analogy. "The family worship table" was a way to describe our multigenerational approach that would help every age-group embrace people at different points on the age continuum. We didn't know it was as special as it was. And it did not come without difficulty.

The commitment to use Sundays as a gathering place for the "family worship table" began when I started thinking about how to integrate fresh faces and young hearts into the leadership of worship at New Life Church. We made a shift in our church to remain musically relevant, and I struggled to help people understand what we were doing. New Life had always been a charismatic church theologically, but our style and culture had stagnated. We were thriving spiritually but hadn't progressed in our expression artistically or musically. I had arrived during year six of the church, and now it was twelve years old. The church continued to grow, and we built the foundations of a successful worship ministry with strong musicians and biblical teaching, but we weren't moving culturally at the speed we needed to. I recruited some young college graduates to inject life into our ministry and help chart the course ahead.

I began to articulate the idea of a family, and the Lord's Table and the Last Supper were the obvious context. The idea of the family worship table came together as we welcomed young people into the planning process. Slowly, we began to change and experience genuine multigenerational worship. New Life was a thriving and healthy church, but as we began to change musically and artistically, the process uncovered poor attitudes and selfishness in some who had been there for a while. Some of the family did not want to actually invite the kids to the table. They wanted them to stay at their own kids' table. They wanted them to do their own music and have their own liturgy so that they could keep things comfortable and clean. They wanted no mess, no fuss—they just wanted to enjoy their own church services.

THE KIDS' TABLE

Many of our churches have decided to stop having family dinners. We've relegated young people to the kids' table because it's easier that way. All the kids eating at the table with the grown-ups is messy, and it's just too much work. It creates awkward moments. There's always such a mess to clean up. It's incredibly inconvenient and requires so much effort from the older and more mature members of the family. Grandma and Grandpa can only take so much noise, you know. Parents are busy with preparation and hosting. Teenagers feel more comfortable with their own kind anyway, and frankly, that relieves most parents and grandparents for a couple of hours on a Sunday morning.

Sadly, many of our churches have adopted this philosophy as a weekly practice, segmenting the family and trying to meet each individual family member's needs in a separate, systematic, and orderly way. Many churches approach ministry to people through the lens of an educational system instead of through the analogy of the family. This single paradigm has had a profound, and not necessarily positive, effect on our twenty-first-century American church life.

Instead of the organic sharing of an experience, we have opted to niche market the church experience to each unique demographic. Instead of creating a broad multigenerational culture, we segment the church into individualistic cultures, each tailor-made for our preferences, tastes, and enjoyment. A meal is a multisensory encounter with many complementary tastes, smells, textures, and dialogues. Many of our churches have opted for a perfect regurgitation of information instead of a messy encounter that actually results in transformation. The family meal is interactive, communal, and provides the perfect illustration of God's family of believers.

GENERATIONAL WORSHIP

Worship is not the only area of disagreement between the generations in the church, but it is the most obvious one. It is one of the most public elements that dominate the landscape of the church and help define its culture. Worship styles and preferences are many and varied, and have come to determine large segments of our theology of worship. Some Presbyterians, Lutherans, and Methodists retain a high-church liturgy, while Baptists, Pentecostals, and charismatics are often purveyors of low-church liturgy, but all denominations have to wrestle with how to worship in an intergenerational way.

The fight has been going a long time. A prominent American pastor compiled this list of complaints regarding new music in the church:

1. It's too new, like an unknown language.
2. It's not so melodious as the more established style.
3. There are so many new songs that it is impossible to learn them all.
4. This new music creates disturbances and causes people to act in an indecent and disorderly manner.
5. It places too much emphasis on instrumental music rather than on godly lyrics.
6. The lyrics are often worldly, even blasphemous.
7. It is not needed, since preceding generations have gone to heaven without it.
8. It is a contrivance to get money.
9. It monopolizes the Christians' time and encourages them to stay out late.
10. These new musicians are young upstarts, and some of them are lewd and loose persons.

The ten reasons above were adapted from a 1723 statement directed against the use of hymns![1] Worship can be controversial indeed and always results in an opinion because it is so influential, culture shaping, and, I believe, spiritual. Worship is about giving glory to God, connecting with God, and ultimately, engaging with Him.

A multigenerational approach is needed in marriage ministries as older couples coach younger couples. The student ministries need older adults who will connect with young men and women as they grow. Children's ministries are often in need of volunteers because the work is so demanding, and often only one generation gives its time, attention, and effort to training, encouraging, and caring for children. Doing church is definitely an intergenerational ministry. But nothing replaces worship as the catalyst for multigenerational discussions. We're not just interested in serving young people's needs; we also need to honor our older brothers and sisters in Christ and meet their needs as well.

CONTENT VS. PERSONNEL

At New Life Church in the late 1990s and early 2000s, we changed our musical style and cultural setting with new paint, lighting, and other cosmetic updates, but the power of what we did was not based in the aesthetics but in the people.

People are always the key to changing a culture. It's not the content of the music or the best and most current material that will convince people they need to let go of the style they've become most comfortable with. Many churches have focused on new songs, new content, and cosmetics as a way of updating, when they should have been inviting the next generation into the discussion. Instead of old people singing new songs, we find power in letting young people participate. Instead of young people just supporting the gathering musically, we need to let them lead once in a while, and also demonstrate to our church how to follow.

Some churches like to invite the youth worship team to lead worship in "Big" church once a year, and if that is all your church can do to integrate, wonderful. That's a start. Keep moving forward so that the next generation feels valued and the older generations feel honored. But ultimately we've got to bring the family together. Once a year is not enough for the family culture to coalesce around the same values and vision.

New Life Church made it through our transition of music, style, and cosmetics because I stood right in the middle of it. I was the older brother, the coach and mentor working with the young men and women who led with me every Sunday. At first it was sporadic, but then we became more consistent in having young people playing, singing, and leading. When a young person messed up or did something awkward, I was right there to pick it up and help. I was a safety net for them *and* for the congregation.

Some Sundays I'd take more risks than other Sundays, but we kept moving toward an integration of the family. One of the keys to healthy change is knowing when to take risks and when to hold steady. Everyone was coming to the table to share, to be fed, and to worship together. Slowly, we began to embrace the entire family.

WHO SETS THE CULTURE AT DINNER?

Every church has a culture, just like every family has a culture. It's the atmosphere that goes unnoticed to all the members but not to the guests who come over for dinner. I liken it to a scent that is not your own. Don't act like you don't know what I'm talking about. All of us have visited another family's house for dinner and walked into a smell that is not our own, that is not familiar. Culture permeates our services, our offices, our small groups, our worship, our prayers, and our before- and after-church gatherings.

I know culture is tricky because as a church planter, I am in the process of creating a culture in every area of our ministry. I'm trying to convey values and principles for the first time every time we do something new. If I try too hard, then it ends up feeling heavy handed and pressurized. The church can easily become synthetic and sterile. People will cooperate, but it's not natural. If I don't try to create culture at all, there will be no leadership, and people will do whatever they want. Come to think of it, this is probably what kills a lot of church plants—the pastor is too heavy on the culture or too light.

Sunday is a big culture-creating day in the life of a church. I like to call it our "family worship table," when the whole family gets together, loving and serving one another. Now, we don't spend all week together. We each have our separate activities just like a real family. My kids don't spend all day with me; instead, they go to school, or they go to play outside, or they go over to a friend's house. But then we all come back together, most days of the week, for a family dinner around the table.

We did it tonight at the Parsley home. We had barbecue brisket sandwiches, potato casserole, and green beans. We talked about the last week of school. Each of the kids told a story, Ethan kept interrupting and talking, and Owen kept jumping up and down from his seat to get his toys. Grace had problems with her new spacers that she just got from the dentist to prepare for braces. Zachary kept making fun of Ethan, and Taylor tried to make the case for why he shouldn't have to go to school for the next two days since he doesn't have any more finals to take. It was a pretty typical dinner—not pretty, but good conversation and nourishment. We are in the midst of creating culture.

Sundays are the time when our church family comes together. We have a high-school group meeting on Wednesday evenings, a college meeting on Mondays, and other events for the older saints in our congregation. We train the children in separate classes, but we come together every week to share our lives with the family.

Sundays are a time to demonstrate that we belong to something bigger than ourselves. It is the defining meeting of our week as a community of Christ. We come together and eat, so to speak, then share conversation, encouragement, challenge, and correction. It is a family day that teaches the next generation that we all belong at the table.

At ONEchapel, we bring our middle-school and high-school students into our main services. Children go to separate classes up to fifth grade, and then we invite them to join us in the fellowship of adults at ages twelve and thirteen. There is a rite of passage here that we want to honor and capitalize on as these young men and women join us in what I like to call "Big Church." Children of all ages are welcome in any service that their parents want them in, and we all gather every fifth Sunday for what we call "Family Sunday," where all of the littlest children are in the auditorium with all of the adults. This can get pretty crazy with distractions and a low-level hum in the room, but I teach our congregation to welcome these little ones and to let them come to Jesus.

We typically create special elements for this service that keep all of the family engaged. We especially encourage moms that we don't mind the noise or the in-and-out that comes with little kids in the service. Moms get the most nervous because it seems to fall to them to quiet and comfort much as they do on an airplane where they have to deal with hundreds of onlookers. We tell everybody that we don't mind because this is our family and we all need to learn how to worship together. We're all experiencing, engaging, and loving one another in very practical ways. Everyone gets it and happily partici-pates. Each Sunday we provide age-specific childcare classes up to fifth grade, and invite middle-school students to join the adults. This keeps us pretty focused on a wide crosssection of experiences and perspectives. It helps me communicate to young people as the pastor and challenges all of us who are older to recognize that the young people are an important part of our community and welcome at the family worship table.

But who actually sets the culture at the family dinner table? Most of us want to say that Dad sets the culture. He's in charge as the man of the house, and he lays down the rules. Right? You would like to think so, wouldn't you? Others think it's Mom because if Momma ain't happy, then nobody's happy. But they're wrong too. The people who set the culture at the dinner table are the kids! Not because they're in charge or completely spoiled, but because just by the act of being there at the table, they determine what kind of culture is being created. It is the difference between having all adults together, and a mixture of adults and kids together—two completely different settings, two unique dinner conversations, and two fundamentally distinctive cultures.

Here's what I mean. I'm in the process of helping my boys under-stand how to have manners at the table. No elbows on the table, no whistling, no beating on your brother at the table, you know, all the standard stuff. My boys are at the age when they think everything gross is funny, so I'm teaching them how not to talk about boogers and farts at the table. Just the fact that I have to correct them, lead them through the conversation, and coach them on how to treat one another means that they are influencing the culture at the dinner table. Young people create the culture of our tables, our churches, and our country. Whether we like it or not, it is fundamentally true. But our job as parents is to raise them—to influence them and give them our hearts. With my boys, I have to lean in toward them to help them understand, obey, and follow my instructions.

Youth culture influences American culture as in no other country in the world. We all want to be young and will pay practically any price to look younger than we are. As age sets in, we find a lack of inclusion, acknowledgment, and sometimes respect. But grandparents should not just retire and play golf; they need to pass down values, lessons, and family heritage. It is our responsibility, as parents, to train, encourage, and connect our children to our family story. Young people today are often so rootless because of divorce and the lack of parental involvement that they have no basis on which to make decisions. They don't get guidance and they don't ask for it; not just because they don't want to, but because there's no one there to ask.

TWO WAYS TO HAVE DINNER

Now, I can have dinner in a couple of different ways. Have you ever heard the motto "Children are to be seen and not heard"?

Some parents just want their kids to sit down, shut up, and eat their green beans. They treat their children and teenagers with a harshness and an authority that crush them, kill their imaginations, smother their sense of wonder, and most damagingly, cause them to hate dinner with the family. Then they'll find any excuse they can to eat at a friend's house—anything not to have to endure the family meal.

I know some churches that function like this toward the next generation. They may give young people a place at the table, but then they make sure the young people know who is in charge. The church leaders want them to be quiet and not make too much noise. "Don't ruin the carpet, and don't use our stuff because you'll just destroy it," they say. These adults don't invite them as much as tolerate them at the table. Then they wonder where the young people go as they grow up. But there is another way to have family dinner that captures the imaginations of the young: encouraging, directing, and coaching them all through the meal.

I love to laugh at our dinner table. I like my kids to tell a story about their day at school or share something that happened to them that day. In the midst of it, I join them in their story, coaching them, challenging them, and correcting them if things get out of hand. It all has to happen at the same time. It is hard work, and I don't always feel like doing it, and frankly, I'm not always successful. But then, that's part of it too, isn't it? The family table is not perfect, sterile, or forced. It's real, organic, authentic, and a bit messy. It's inconvenient and challenging to me as a parent, but absolutely necessary and incredibly rewarding. In fact, it forces me to be the mature adult God wants me to be, teaching me to fully love my kids.

WHO SETS THE CULTURE FOR SUNDAYS?

If our Sunday church services are the dinner events for our church family, then it follows that the kids and teenagers are going to end up influencing the church culture in a dramatic way. If we're going to gather everyone together for dinner, then we've got to allow our kids to join in with us in conversations and questions. We've got to include them and interact with them with all of our effort and energy. It is the act of leaning toward them instead of away from them. That might mean more music that reflects their culture rather than yours. It might mean being willing to surrender to new cultural norms in our church services. No doubt, we must pass our values on to them, but we also need to make sure that they love dinnertime instead of dread it. It won't be easy or convenient, but it will be rewarding as they grow up and learn what it means to sacrifice and share their lives with others.

Here are a few ideas to get you moving in the right direction, but remember, you have to change people's mind-sets in order for this culture to take hold. That means modeling, teaching, and training.

CREATING A SUNDAY-MORNING FAMILY CULTURE

1. Include youth leaders on your Sunday-morning worship teams.

When a high-school student arrives with his parents on Sunday morning and sees the same guy who led the Wednesday-night youth worship fully engaged in leading adults in worship, he is more likely to value the service. When students see "their guy" helping facilitate worship, it gives them a model to follow as well as confidence that their generation is valued and embraced in Big Church. Sometimes this is a logistical struggle because of scheduling or focus, but the dividends are worth the extra investment. If your youth meetings are on Sunday morning, change their meeting times. Get the youth pastor and the worship leader working together, not separately, and why not have the youth worship leader lead a hymn once in a while? I'll never forget the first time I let Jon Egan, the New Life student ministries worship leader at the time, lead a guitar-laden version of "Nothing but the Blood of Jesus." It was awesome!

Undo the stereotype, and be sure that you encourage an atmosphere of cooperation and coaching in the worship team. The worship leader needs to invest in a relationship with these young leaders and begin to reproduce himself or herself in others. For some the concept needs to be reversed, and there needs to be older and more mature adults leading in worship on the stage and not just a bunch of kids trying to lead all the adults. This can be challenging for a young leader, but worth the effort to change the church culture to a family environment.

2. Make sure the song selections overlap with student services.

It's well documented that many twentysomethings go through a period of disillusionment and disappear from our churches. One of the reasons is the weekly college meeting often bears no resemblance whatsoever to the Sunday-morning service, and the transition from one to the other is difficult. These young people graduate and move up to Big Church only to find a completely different landscape. The radical difference shouts, "You're not welcome here!" They get lost and conclude there is nothing for them in this service, and furthermore, no one will notice if they disappear. And most of the time, no one does. However, when they recognize something familiar, they have a chance to connect with the service, and with God. We've got to make sure student services dabble with the arrangements of older songs, including hymns, and that the Big Church leaders are experimenting with modern worship songs. You don't have to sing all the same songs, but there should be healthy overlap. The best thing Glenn Packiam, our college-ministry worship leader, did to help this process was to sing powerful arrangements of hymns that we would also sing in Big Church. He purposely encouraged history and heritage in the college meeting, which meant that there was less pressure on the Big Church gathering to force "older" material.

3. Invite creative input from young people.

It's very common to find young people involved in the Sunday-morning worship ministry in churches across the country. What is unique is allowing those young people to provide leadership in the creativity, planning, and implementation of Big Church worship services. Don't give away the whole service or just host a special occasion where "the youth" lead the worship, rather, actually include them in the process. Don't just *use* them because they're good musicians. *Invest* in them, and allow them to help shape the culture of your church. If you continue to provide leadership, offering guidance and security for the congregation, and you're willing to take the risk to ensure the vibrancy and longevity of your church by encouraging young leaders now, you'll have no problem connecting the next generation to Big Church.

4. Include an older or ancient element in your services.
We're not just interested in young people connecting with God; we want older family members to connect with Him as well. That's why at ONEchapel we sing a hymn or a song that's at least twenty years old in *every* Sunday-morning service. We also include Communion with corporate prayers, confession, or a creed every Sunday right smack-dab in the middle of our modern worship songs. This is important, not just because it serves our older constituency—that's a consumer way of thinking—but because it educates younger people about the history and heritage of Christianity. They belong to something bigger than themselves, and this way they discover where they're going in their journey of faith by knowing where their Christian family came from. It is the job of parents and grandparents to help raise them, but we need to serve the entire family and not just the next generation in order to truly be multigenerational.

HISTORY, HERITAGE, AND LEGACY

I believe this final idea is an essential component of the family worship table. The responsibility of parents and grandparents is to make sure that their values, traditions, lessons, and stories are passed down to their kids and grandkids. Perpetuating the family name used to be a bigger deal than it is today, but I believe that when we look at a church's longevity and the goal of next-generation leadership, we are dealing not just with ideas, but with resources and wisdom as well.

How will a young teenage boy learn anything about his grandfather if he never has to sit across from him at the dinner table? How will a young girl understand her grandmother's legacy if she never listens to a story, even though it might go on and on? How will older adults retain their vibrancy in life without anyone to whom they can pass on their wisdom?

There is nothing sadder than older people who have lost their will to live because they've run out of purpose. We see it when the spouse of an older person dies and often it's not long until that person passes away too. Why? Many times, it's because in losing his spouse he's lost his reason for living. It is my conviction that our older saints need the energy and enthusiasm of the younger generation to keep them vibrant in their old age. An older believer is recharged when she's pouring into a young person, mentoring a young couple, or involved in facilitating ministry to the next generation. She comes alive with renewed purpose and vision.

Some churches have sold out to be so relevant to the next generation that they no longer have room at the table for anyone who is older and wiser. I know of one church in which the pastor stood up and said, "We're changing things around here to reach the next generation, so if you don't like the songs or the way we're singing them, then you can just leave." And some did! We didn't choose that route at ONEchapel. We chose to honor those who came before us and to learn the lessons of what came before us. We chose to include our elders and share in the history of their songs, their creeds, and their prayers. We're better for it!

Like my grandparents' breakfast, there is warmth, comfort, protection, and love in our family gatherings at ONEchapel. Everyone knows that we're leaning toward the next generation while at the same time continuing to honor the generation that came before us. We must have both heritage and innovation. We need to know our history as well as the mystery of the work of the Holy Spirit among us now.

Just as we don't want to send the kids away to the kids' table for our own benefit, we do not want to send our grandparents away to the nursing home. We want them at the table, sharing their stories, listening to ours, and giving us wisdom and guidance. I guarantee you that the great-grandparents don't need to be with the kids every moment of the week, but they certainly need to be at the table!

Our churches need to be full of Abrahams, Isaacs, and Jacobs as well!

We need grandpas and grandmas, middle-aged moms and dads, young professionals, teenagers, and kids, to be truly healthy as a family.

We were made for community. We were made to need each other.

What's our motivatiton? Love.

NOTES

1. Bob Sorge, *Exploring Worship: A Practical Guide to Praise and Worship* (Lee's Summit: MO, 1987), 137.

THE DAVID GENERATION

Psalm 145:4 says, "One generation commends your works to another; they tell of your mighty acts."

David, the writer of Psalm 145, understood that it is imperative for one generation to pass on the stories of God's miraculous works so that the next generation won't forget how they have arrived on the scene. David knew that people who have witnessed the faithfulness of God must share these stories with future generations so they won't lose their way, become discouraged, or doubt that God is with them. One generation should not have to learn the same lessons already learned by the generations before them, but should stand firm on the shoulders of those who know the goodness of God.

Across the landscape of our nation we see each generation declaring God's work among themselves, but not enough commending of God's works from one generation to another. We're pretty good at marketing to our niche demographic groups but maybe not so good at sharing God's great deeds in a cross-generational way.

David had a unique perspective on these generational challenges and knew firsthand about the discrimination and resistance generations sometimes have toward one another. He rose from life as a shepherd boy to becoming the most beloved king of Israel, and his journey led him to pen the words of Psalm 145:4 after he, as a young man, made a profound impact on an old war. Indeed, the story is one of the most iconic in our culture and the action for which David is most famous.

Slaying a giant.

The setting for this event is 1 Samuel 17, a time when Israel was under the rule of King Saul. The Philistines were a constant enemy and challenging force, invading Israel early on in the book of 1 Samuel. Samuel was a respected prophet and judge, and the man who led Israel and restored the peace since "the hand of the LORD was against the Philistines" (1 Sam. 7:13) throughout Samuel's lifetime.

God had given them Saul, a tall, handsome, and powerful first king. By this time in the story, Samuel had already rebuked Saul for his disobedience to God and desire for the approval of his people, clarifying for Saul that the Lord rejected him as king and chose another.

Thus, our young hero entered the story as a shepherd boy of no reputation—the youngest of eight boys and no stranger to hard work. He was a musician and poet who was obviously ignored and overlooked by his brothers and father. Overlooked by everyone except God, who chose him to be the next king of Israel based on what was in his heart (1 Sam. 16:7)!

Meanwhile, an "evil spirit" tormented Saul as he bemoaned God's rejection. One of Saul's servants witnessed the talent and skill of David's musicianship, and God's sovereign hand ushered the young shepherd into Saul's service to play the harp for him, to try to keep the evil spirit at bay. David continued to shuttle between shepherding in the fields near his home and playing music for Saul.

At this time, a new twist emerged in the conflict between the Israelites and the Philistines over land and borders, and the two armies camped out facing each other across the Valley of Elah. A champion from Gath, named Goliath, arrived on the scene at nine feet tall, wearing a truckload of armor—and he was the most intimidating force Israel had ever seen.

A FALSE WAR

Goliath showed up after his morning mug of coffee each day and issued a challenge to the Israelite army. He'd taken control of the situation by changing the terms of the war. No longer was this battle about who had the greater army, strategy, or numbers. Goliath intimidated the army and King Saul himself out of any confidence in God or their own ability to fight. There was no battle going on here, only words—*insults and challenges*—terrifying the men of Israel. In fact, Scripture says the men of Israel went out every morning to their battle lines in the valley, "shouting the war cry" (1 Sam. 17:20) until Goliath stepped forward with his usual defiance, at which point the Israelites turned and ran from him "in great fear" (v. 24). As crazy as this seems, it had been going on for forty days!

I see myself in this story, and you might see yourself as well. We often abdicate our role in the battle—we don't fight as much as listen to the Enemy insult us and challenge us to a duel on his terms. Instead of rejecting the new terms, we accept them and allow ourselves to be defined by intimidation and fear. Whether it's our own past failures, a struggle in our relationships, a challenge at work, or financial pressure, instead of believing in God's ability to lead us into battle, we accept the crazy terms of our Enemy and continue to live each day under the fear, anxiety, and guilt of the Enemy's intimidation. David's young heart, cultivated by hours upon hours of prayer, worship, and the challenges faced in the isolation of the sheep fields, knew that these terms must be rejected.

In the twenty-first-century American church, I wonder if we may have similarly abdicated the battle to the realm of intimidation and fear. We have a lot going on in our churches. There is much talking and teaching—even some shouting going on, but is it just noise? There are constant activities and lots of vision, but are we sounding the war cry and then surrendering to the Enemy's terms by not loving our neighbors? Are we secretly paralyzed by our failure to be the people of God that He wants us to be in our cities? Is the divorce rate in the church and the pornography problem among our men keeping us weak and impotent? Are we surrendering ground by believing that no one wants to hear our message? Are we intimidated by fear of rejection and persecution? Are we blinded by those fears? Are we turning away from the answer by segmenting our churches into demographic marketing schemes and thereby appealing to the worst elements of our consumerist culture? Is there a great war cry, but very little kingdom building? All too often the answer is, sadly, yes.

Now back to the story in 1 Samuel.

David arrived at the battle lines, saw this spectacle, and found his brothers unwelcoming. He was sent by his father, Jesse, to bring bread and cheese to his brothers Eliab, Abinadab, and Shammah, and also to bring back some news on how they were doing. Despite this fabulous pizza delivery service (bread and cheese … get it?), his older brothers were somehow resentful of David's presence. Eliab burned with anger after hearing David ask the other men about what King

Saul had promised to the man who would kill Goliath. Eliab replied
to David, "Why have you come down here? And with whom did you
leave those few sheep in the wilderness? I know how conceited you
are and how wicked your heart is; you came down only to watch the
battle" (1 Sam 17:28).

I love David's response: "Now what have I done? … Can't I even
speak?" (v. 29). It sounds so brotherly. I've heard it with my two
brothers growing up, and you can tell that David and Eliab have had
this kind of conversation before.

At first glance, you might think it is just about the embarrassment that Eliab experienced in front of his little brother as he runs
away from Goliath with the rest of the men of Israel. I mean, that
couldn't have felt terribly brave. But there is something more going
on here. There was an event in their history that led Eliab to the con-
clusion that David was conceited and adventurous beyond reason. I
believe Eliab's response might have been because Samuel had passed
over him and his six brothers. They'd stood and waited while David
was brought to Samuel and anointed as the next king of Israel. That
experience occurred just prior to this meeting, and the sting of the
younger brother's promotion above him had to be fresh in Eliab's
mind and emotions.

David responded as any brother would and ignored his older
brother and asked for more clarification from others. David was
interested in the reward, but we find that he was also motivated by
something greater. He was appalled by the way this uncircumcised
Philistine defied the armies of the living God! It was a travesty and
an insult to God's reputation, and David was going to do something
about it!

There is a reason the term "youthful idealism" was coined as a way of describing the naïveté of young people. Age has a way of sobering us. Our experiences, our disappointments, and our failures have a way of shrinking our expectations. Sometimes they wound us in a way that steals our faith and bankrupts our dreams. As a result, we tend to discourage anyone who thinks he or she can overcome the obstacles that have stopped us in the past. It's human nature. But it's not God's nature.

Eliab was resentful of a young whippersnapper who thought he could come in and change the entire situation on his own. He was upset by the bravado, David's seemingly naked ambition and self-confidence. It was offensive to him. Not only was this giant of an enemy insulting him, but now, his little brother had insulted him for his inability to bravely fight. And David was throwing the "God" card around! Eliab heard his little brother say that God should not be treated this way and that this enemy should not be tolerated. Things needed to change, and quick!

Does this sound familiar to anyone?

THE BATTLEGROUND OF WORSHIP

As I listen to the next generation of young leaders, I sometimes feel like I'm in a time warp. As a man in my forties, I'm technically classified as generation X, but I'm old enough to see many similarities between the Jesus Movement of the 1970s and what our young brothers and sisters say about the church today. Our "boomer generation" parents rejected the rigidity of church tradition in America. The boomers were often rejected by many of the established mainline denominations as long-haired hippies, but with their massive numbers it wasn't long before they began to dominate the cultural landscape.

The Jesus Movement generation of the 1970s hungered for authenticity and a genuine demonstration of God's power. Since the mainline church rejected them, they created their own church culture, unencumbered by tradition, which morphed into the mega-church movement of the '80s and '90s. The worship wars of this era became the primary battleground of this generational conflict. Nowhere in the church did we see the battle lines drawn in a clearer way than in our liturgy and music. Many a congregation split over whether or not to use drums in the church, and countless coffee-houses were established in an attempt to deal with the problem of the American church's increasing irrelevance.

Incredibly, we might be repeating history.

Eliab gives us a clear picture of our churches, which tend to resent the next generation and their new ways of thinking. What's wrong with how we've been doing church faithfully for all these years? We sometimes view young people's ideas and enthusiasm for change as naïveté and foolishness. We resent the idea that they think they can just come in and change something that has been going on for a long time, or quickly overcome a challenge that we've wrestled with for years. Who do they think they are anyway?

Well, David was, in fact, the young man who would kill Goliath.

While it may be true that David was overly enthusiastic, or even idealistic, there can be no doubt that he was the one who thought about the situation differently from his older brothers. He brought a new perspective and energy to the equation, and God gave him the innovative idea for how to defeat this enemy. He may have appeared egocentric, but God empowered him because he was motivated to defend God's reputation. He believed God was with him.

And he was right.

Our young friends dubbed the "millennials," those born after 1980, may have the very answers to the problems our churches face. Instead of resentment, we need to embrace them as God's provision in overcoming our Enemy.

Hearing of David's disdain for Goliath, King Saul sent for David and promptly lectured him on his deficiencies: "You're too young, you have no fighting skills, and by the way, Goliath has been a warrior in training since he was your age!" David made his case by telling Saul stories of his shepherding adventures. David also revealed the reason for his confidence and the origin of his plan for killing Goliath. He protected his sheep from both a lion and a bear, experiences that gave him the faith to fight this Philistine.

David was not necessarily conceited—he was confident. This confidence came from the realization that God had delivered him from both a lion and a bear. David's idealism wasn't idealism at all, but a plan rooted in experience, prayer, and faith in God's love and protection. He was convinced that God would deliver him, and God's people, from this Philistine.

King Saul responded by saying, "Go, and the LORD be with you" (1 Sam. 17:37). Which sounds to me like, "I think your odds are zero, but I'd love to see you try. God be with you as you end your life here on earth." Saul tried to give David his own armor so he would literally go out in style. The king's armor was the best there was in the army, and it was a symbol of status and support. However, as David moved around wearing the armor, he realized that he couldn't use it. It was too big and clunky for the lean shepherd boy. He left the armor behind, saying, "I cannot go in these … because I am not used to them" (v. 39). David was not yet a man of war, but he was a man of heart. He knew his limits, and he knew there was another way God wanted to use him.

King Saul did what so many have done. He expected the next generation to win the battle exactly as he had won his battles. Make no mistake: Saul wanted David to have the best. He wanted David to win, but the only way he saw him winning was through his own paradigm. He couldn't imagine another way. He didn't want to punish his young musician who had been such a blessing to him; he wanted to protect him. So, he offered David what he had. Only, it wasn't God's best for David, who had an innovative way of looking at the challenge ahead of him. It was based on his experience and his understanding of God's grace for him. This was the winning combination.

Our churches often do what King Saul did. We try to fit the next generation into our own plans and force them to use the same ideas, tactics, and tools that were used in the past. Sometimes this is rooted in pride or fear, but mostly just because we can't imagine God using a scrawny little teenager to transform the battle. As I learned long ago from one of my mentors, Bob Sorge, the last seven words of a dying church are "We've never done it this way before." We struggle with embracing the innovation, energy, and enthusiasm of our young Davids.

Bill Gates is known for innovation and strategy, and he recognizes that college students and their ideas will lead Microsoft forward. That is why Gates made his company culture conducive to college students, giving them a place to create and innovate. Instead of rejecting them or competing with them, he embraced their creativity and ingenuity, ensuring himself and the company future success. The success of Microsoft is due in large part to this philosophy. The corporate cultures of Google and Facebook are two more examples of this way of thinking, which allows for the expression of young minds, encouraging and validating them as valuable to their organizations. Unfortunately, our churches aren't always so welcoming.

We must not be like David's resentful older brother, or the myopic King Saul, but rather, willing to embrace the next generation's ideas and innovation to further validate and invigorate the lives of our churches. We will strengthen our family of believers if we aren't overly protective of our own success and defensive of the way we've always done things.

The "millenial generation" is the largest generation ever in America and we must all look to the future examining and planning how the next generation will take hold of leadership within the American church. How well this transition happens depends on how well we obey Psalm 145. This issue requires us to embrace the very building blocks of a family: love, cooperation, respect, humility, and innovation as the family grows.

These are the values of every healthy family that will help our church families slay the giant that keeps the generations apart. I like to think of them as five smooth stones.

FIVE SMOOTH STONES

1. Family

In our divorce culture, the idea of family is more important than ever. Building healthy, strong, and secure family churches means inviting every age to participate. Contrary to some opinions, I believe that one of the greatest desires of the millennials is to *belong*. They want to be rooted, connected, and celebrated within a family. If we will see our churches as families instead of consumer warehouses, we'll produce better materials, creativity, and solutions in the church. Living together in a multigenerational family with fathers and sons, mothers and daughters, grandparents and grandkids would create security, stability, and longevity within our churches that would empower the next generation to great exploits with confidence and courage.

2. Cooperation

I've seen many college groups and young-adult ministries splitting off from a more mature and established church to build their own churches. Instead, I believe the church needs to adopt a symbiotic relationship between older and younger believers to accomplish all that God wants in this generation. Consider this: Wouldn't it be incredible if we could take the *maturity*, *wisdom*, and *resources* of age and put them together with the *energy*, *enthusiasm*, and *creativity* of youth? Our churches would be an unstoppable force in our communities. This kind of synergy makes the church more relevant than ever. If we could harness the strengths of both old and young, of experience and innovation, and of hindsight and foresight, we could change the world. There is nothing we couldn't do. We would have all that we need to accomplish the purposes of God in our generation.

3. Respect

In order for different generations to share cooperation and innovation, there must be mutual respect. This collaboration begins with a healthy respect for heritage and history. Those who ignore history are bound to repeat it. Knowing where we come from is just as important as knowing where we're going—in fact, these are interconnected concepts that provide wisdom and revelation. Young men and women need history and heritage so that they will know who they are and learn from past mistakes and successful ventures that can propel them into the future. However, the older generation must also respect their younger colaborers by allowing them to give input, carry responsibility, and accept a place at the table where new ideas and creativity can improve our effectiveness as the church. Respect means that you honor and encourage the gifts God has given to a person or group of people—an indispensable character trait for intergenerational cooperation.

4. Humility

First Peter 5:5–6 says that young men should be submissive to those who are older, but the next line also says that we should clothe ourselves with humility. This means none of us can afford to think more highly of ourselves than we ought to. We must not buy into the lie that those who are older have nothing to offer the landscape of ministry, nor can we afford to dismiss our younger siblings because of some perceived idealism or inexperience. We can all learn something if we're willing to remain humble. We can't learn everything from someone, but we can learn something from everyone. Humility opens the door to new ideas and ancient truths and provides the glue that bonds a multigenerational family.

5. Innovation

The most significant impact the next generation will have on the church of tomorrow may be through their technological creativity. In a placeless society where virtual relationships are a way of life, we're going to continue to see more innovation in the way the church connects, communicates, and creates community. Every generation must resist the temptation to hold on to the way ministry happened in the past. God always works within our cultural distinctiveness through ancient truths. Methods must always yield to cultural change while the bedrock of a timeless message remains immovable. Instead of resisting, the older generation must embrace new ideas while bringing their wisdom and experience to the table. The church needs a new way of innovating, and that way includes more than just one generation.

In one sense, we must not make too big a deal out of the changes we're experiencing in the church in America. I mean, let's face it, no one is surprised when a college sophomore thinks she's stumbled onto a totally new idea, only to realize a few years later that every generation has wrestled with its own hunger for "authenticity." You just have to smile when you think about it. It's innocent. It's ideal-istic. *And it's wonderful.* Dr. Mark Roberts wrote a poignant article called "Millennials" in *Worship Leader* magazine a few years ago that taps into this cyclical idea that those in each generation move "to the comfortable middle" as they get older and then ultimately feel "the sting of being passé."[1]

What removes the sting? What helps guide the idealism of a twentysomething? In a word, *love.* Parents who love their kids, kids who love their parents, and grandparents who sacrifice for their grandkids because they love them! Love and sacrifice are required if we are going to listen to each other's music in church and embrace one another as a family.

When we surrender to one another and embrace one another regardless of age, culture, or style, something amazing happens.

Mentoring. Creativity. Presence. Authenticity!

When we practice church as family, what was once known as the generation gap disappears. We may wrestle with generational differences, but we have a chance to anticipate and collaborate like never before. We don't have to repeat history. We don't have to reject what came before us or what's happening now.

The signs encourage me. I have great hope for the church in North America, but I do not believe any single generation can do it alone. There is a great need for a multigenerational approach—one generation proclaiming God's mighty works to another—Psalm 145.

We need many more older and seasoned believers who are willing to mentor and encourage the gifts in our young men and women without trying to put their own armor on the younger generation as Saul did to David. We also have a generation of young Davids who are ready to fight alongside their older, more experienced brothers if only we will invite them, embrace them, and learn from them.

We won't win the battle ahead without each generation sharing with others the great exploits that God has done among them!

NOTES

1. Mark Roberts, "Millennials," *Worship Leader*, September 2007.

Chapter 6

LEARNING WHILE LEADING

The story of David and Goliath stands as one of many illustrations of how God is willing to use people who we think are not ready for prime-time ministry. Throughout Scripture we find story after story of God working through flawed, failed, or foolish young men and women. Consider Jeremiah, the young prophet who spoke the words of God (Jer. 1:1–10); Timothy, the young apprentice of Paul the apostle (1 Tim. 4:12); Gideon, who was the least in his tribe (Judg. 6:1–32), and Josiah, the boy king who ruled in righteousness (2 Kings 22–23). They faced the challenges of inexperience, lack of courage, and lack of others' confidence. God spoke to each of them directly and asked them to do something that seemed beyond their years. The message in each of these stories is clear: God can use anybody! I know it's true because as a young man I received the love, support, and encouragement of more than one leader who took a risk on me.

One of them is a brilliant pastor whom I served under named Dr. David S. Bishop. Pastor Bishop, as I knew him, was a thoughtful, meticulous man and a great communicator whose hair always stood perfectly in place. Don't get me wrong; he wasn't uptight. He was not the kind of man who demanded perfection, but he was the kind of man who put the fear of God in you while making you feel both loved and safe at the same time. This man took a risk by letting a nineteen-year-old kid lead worship in a very influential church of eight hundred people.

My dad and stepmom began a new life together by attending Christian Life Center in Yakima, Washington, with four of their six children. I moved into the house of our new blended family just after my nineteenth birthday. A few months earlier, Pastor Bishop had married my dad and stepmom, so he knew that our family was in the process of making a new start in a new city with a new church. As we began to serve around the church, I was asked to lead worship for the youth group.

I still remember the day that worship pastor Larry Lee called and asked me to fill in for him, leading worship for Big Church while he was gone. I was a little nervous and intimidated, but very excited to move up to the "big leagues."

I was such a skinny, scrawny little teenager, who looked more like he was fourteen years old than nineteen, but my voice was good and my heart innocent. That's about all I had going for me. The pianist and mother of three, Gwen Shipley, helped me figure it out and supported me musically, while the drummer, eighteen-year-old Scott Steinloski, put up with my crazy signals. However, in that service, and in many others, we worshipped Jesus. I started into regular rotation on Sunday mornings, and it was the beginning of my development as a worship leader. I wasn't always smooth, I didn't know how to encourage the congregation, and I was probably a little overly energetic. But I'll always be grateful for men like David S. Bishop who invested in my life at a pivotal moment.

Creating opportunities for young and inexperienced leaders is one of the most effective tools we have to continue to make the church dynamic and relevant in our culture. Helping young leaders is extremely challenging because it demands accountability, it involves some risk, and it can be downright messy; but it is indispensable to a church that is committed to longevity. Every good organization knows that one of the secrets to long-term success is the constant development of young talent. Our churches need to embrace this idea in a much more intentional and direct manner.

Now that I'm well into my forties, I'm convinced that we need to allow people to learn while they lead. Learning while leading is probably closer to the model Jesus used with His disciples than most of what we're doing now in our traditional American churches. I know that there are many good church plants and other youth movements happening around the country, but not enough partnerships that include a multigenerational approach for growing leaders.

If you think about it, we're at the transitional crossroads for many of the megachurches that were started in America in the late '70s and '80s as they approach the twenty-five- or thirty-year anniversary mark. They began with energetic and innovative young leaders, and now they're approaching a leadership shift. The question for these churches is did they raise up leaders who can lead the church into the next season, or do they need to hire a headhunter to go find a CEO to take over the ministry?

This question of experience, leadership, and training goes deeper into the development of our church cultures. If we've surrendered to a corporate culture with a "type A" personality at the helm, the search for the next leader often looks different from how it does if we have developed a family culture with leadership modeling and training at its core.

Instead of critiquing our current American models, it's probably much more helpful to look straight at how Jesus encouraged young, undisciplined, and self-absorbed men ... all of whom were handpicked by Him!

JESUS CULTURE

Jesus wasn't afraid to invest in young, energetic people. He didn't choose the brightest of the class or the most academically astute. He didn't choose the most talented or the best looking. He took risks with twelve disciples, and His success rate wasn't bad: eleven out of twelve!

But seriously, Jesus wasn't looking for leaders He could turn into servants. He was looking for servants who would be willing to develop into leaders. He took raw, undisciplined, unschooled, and ordinary men; and they became world changers. A famous leadership axiom is "Leaders aren't born; they are made." We have the privilege of watching the process unfold before our eyes in the Scriptures as Jesus begins to mold these men into disciples. It wasn't easy. It was actually quite messy.

Luke 9 provides stunning insight into this concept.

At the beginning of the chapter, Dr. Luke explained that Jesus called the twelve disciples together and gave them power and authority to drive out all demons and to cure diseases. He sent them out to preach the kingdom of God and to heal the sick. After some brief coaching and encouragement, Scripture says in Luke 9:6 that "they set out and went from village to village, proclaiming the good news and healing people everywhere."

Here, in the midst of this miraculous activity, we find the empowered yet astonishingly petty disciples asking Jesus to send the crowds away to get some food. They were somewhat annoyed by the masses of broken, needy people who followed them around everywhere. They just wanted some alone time with Jesus.

In typical fashion, Jesus challenged the disciples to give the crowd some food themselves, to use what they had (five loaves and two fish) and to mix it with their faith. Jesus's compassion in that situation amazingly lead to five thousand people eating their fill.

A few verses later, Jesus revealed Himself as the Messiah to Peter, James, and John so they would have confidence to face the difficult days ahead. In the moment of transfiguration, Peter could only stick his foot in his mouth by asking to create a shelter to house Jesus's glory. Peter was caught up in the moment and wanted to stay on the mountain and build a place to live. Luke actually described how disoriented Peter was by telling us that he didn't know what he was saying.

Later in this chapter, we observe the inability of the disciples to cast out a demon. Jesus came to their rescue, cast out the demon, and then coached them to increase their spiritual authority by prayer and fasting.

After this, an argument broke out among the disciples over who was the greatest. Jesus chided them and told them that the least among them was the greatest. The disciples just weren't getting it.

Finally, James and John, the "Sons of Thunder," asked Jesus if they should call down fire from heaven to destroy those Samaritans who didn't welcome Jesus to the village they were visiting. Jesus told them not to do it. These are the same guys who were healing people everywhere, right?

The disciples were ambitious and untrained, but incredibly, Jesus gave them power and authority to do the same things that He did.

He let them do miraculous work! Even though they weren't entirely ready, Jesus allowed them to learn while leading.

ON-THE-JOB TRAINING

Many churches have a difficult time embracing this idea. Their systems and structures are built on teaching, learning, and absorbing information. There's only one problem: the kingdom of God does not function on information alone. First Corinthians 4:20 says, "The kingdom of God is not a matter of talk but of power." Learning and growing in Christ have a teaching element, but it must be paired with powerful real-life leadership experiences of sharing God's kingdom with others.

Our own tendency is to demand more training, coaching, and instruction for our young leaders until we finally feel comfortable with them. *Then* they can do something significant for God. This paradigm may keep our churches from benefiting from the energy, enthusiasm, and innovation that we need to remain effective in our quickly changing cultural landscape.

Some Christian leaders have surrendered to the fear and insecurity of this information-only ministry mind-set. They want to know all of the answers before the questions are asked. However, even Jesus told us that He said only what His Father told Him to say, which is impressive for the fully divine Son of God. If anyone could have shared what He knew, it was Jesus. But He didn't. He listened to His Father and then spoke His Father's words. Jesus acted on His Father's instructions. He submitted completely. He ministered to people from a platform of relationship with His heavenly Father, not a platform of conveying information.

In Acts 3–4, Peter and John healed a crippled beggar who was sitting near the entrance of the temple. Peter and John told him that they didn't have any money to give, but what they had, they would gladly offer him.

Then Peter took the beggar by the hand to help him up as he said, "In the name of Jesus Christ of Nazareth, walk." Instantly, the man's feet and ankles became strong, and he began walking and jumping, praising God all around the temple. People were amazed!

Some, however, were not amused. The religious leaders did not like the fact that Peter and John were giving credit to Jesus, the One who had been resurrected from death to life. So the leaders threw Peter and John in jail to spend the night. The next day Peter and John continued to proclaim the message of Christ, and Acts 4:13 says,

> When they saw the courage of Peter and John and
> realized that they were unschooled, ordinary men,
> they were astonished and they took note that these
> men had been with Jesus.

Praying for people to be healed and set free from their sin doesn't really have anything to do with a title, education, talent, or even saying all the right words. It is about the presence of God in us—it is about being *with* Jesus! You don't have to be a certain age or have a certain degree.

Haven't you ever wondered why new believers are typically the most excited about sharing the good news of the gospel with their friends? They've just discovered the wonder of a relationship with the God of the universe.

The world is new.

They are reborn.

Their faith transforms their outlook on life. Anything is possible for these young followers of Christ! They've experienced the greatest of all miracles, and they have to tell someone else about it.

Should we forbid them from speaking into the lives of others just because they are not adequately trained? How much doctrine does it take to receive salvation? Not much. Salvation is more rooted in knowing a person than in knowing theology.

Don't get me wrong here—study and learning are critically important factors for those of us who've been called into the fellowship of Christ. Bible study is valuable and necessary. The Holy Scriptures provide a road map and a record of God's interaction with humanity. Great teaching will always be essential to growth and spiritual maturity. But studying the Scriptures *without* a revelation of Jesus will result in a dead end.

Jesus said as much in John 5:39–40, when He confronted the religious leaders who were trying to trap Him. He told them,

> You study the Scriptures diligently because you
> think that in them you have eternal life. These are
> the very Scriptures that testify about me, yet you
> refuse to come to me to have life.

In this passage, Jesus challenged the belief that all you need to do is study the Scriptures. The Pharisees did that more deeply and effectively than anyone else, but Jesus said it clearly—the Scriptures point to Him, and unless you are willing to embrace Him, you will not receive eternal life! *Jesus* is eternal life. He is the way, the truth, and the life!

The Christian life is not about the transfer of information; it is about a relationship with Jesus. Study is helpful and learning is necessary on our journey of faith, but relationship with Jesus is what fuels our ministry to others. This means that everyone in the family of God is capable of great exploits and miracles.

My missionary friend Britt Hancock believes this to his core. He works with indigenous people groups in the mountains of Mexico where almost no one has anything more than a rudimentary education. He told me a story about one of his disciples, a man who has no more than a second-grade education. This man prayed over his dead grandson for several hours and saw him miraculously rise from the dead!

This story circulated through the village and brought more people to Christ and gave this man the authority and confidence that no education could. I don't know the secret to raising people from the dead, and I don't think this mountain-dwelling descendant of the Aztecs does either. However, I do believe he knows something about being with Jesus!

That's how these young fishermen, tax collectors, and blue-collar disciples could follow Jesus and do the things that He did. The question for us is this: What do young, inexperienced leaders need as immature believers-in-training?

THE RELATIONAL QUOTIENT

Young leaders need more than instruction, they require relational mentoring. They need constant coaching and encouragement. They need correction and redirection that will wear us out. And this mentoring happens best in the context of doing ministry together as friends, fathers, mothers, and disciple makers who will walk through life with them. Relationship is the best context for knowledge transfer. Even Jesus didn't function primarily from a knowledge base in His life and ministry. He spoke and acted out of His relationship with His heavenly Father. That relationship directed Him and gave Him the confidence to do the marvelous works that His Father had in mind for Him to accomplish.

While I was the worship pastor at New Life Church in Colorado Springs, I had the opportunity to encourage and mentor several young worship leaders. These young men had exceptional talent, love for Jesus, and good parents, so they had a great head start on their way to success in ministry. I was privileged to walk with them in their younger years, and since that time, they have all become influential authors, musicians, and leaders in their own right.

I am grateful for Glenn Packiam, who is a fantastic author, a great songwriter, and is now a very effective pastor at New Life Church. But, as a twenty-two-year-old, Glenn was full of his own ideas, ambition, and desire to lead people. Don't get me wrong. Glenn wanted to serve Jesus and people as well; it just tended to get drowned out sometimes by his youthful enthusiasm for influence.

At the time, the worship department at New Life was housed in the World Prayer Center, which is a separate building on the New Life campus. It has a walk of the nations, which is a sidewalk around the circumference of the building with the flags of many nations flying from flagpoles. It is a great place to pray or to talk with a young man in need of encouragement.

Glenn and I had many talks walking around the World Prayer Center. It got to where he knew what was coming if I came to him and said, "Hey, Glenn, let's take a walk." During one particular season early on, Glenn had trouble being on time. It seemed as if he could not arrive on time no matter how much I challenged him.

Finally, it came to a head when we were scheduled to play for an early morning men's meeting at the World Prayer Center that was being simulcast across the country. Five a.m. was the call time, and Glenn was nervous about being late, so he arranged to stay overnight at the WPC in one of the long-term prayer rooms. Unfortunately, I didn't know that he had spent the night in the building. Five a.m. came and went … and no Glenn. We sound checked, and just before we started, someone said, "Glenn should be here. He stayed the night so he wouldn't be late."

We called up to the room, and sure enough, he had overslept.

It was at this moment that the hard truth came alive to him. I told him if he was not able to be on time and honor his commitments, then he could not lead. Other people relied on him, and they would not respect him if he would not respect their time. He could play music, write songs, and do other things, but if this area of his life could not be brought into line, then he would not be able to lead and work for the church.

This defining moment impacted Glenn's life. He committed to punctuality and changed his habits. His work ethic transformed, and the discipline of leadership began to emerge. I knew it was in him; it just took the right set of circumstances to get through to him.

The lesson here is in the process: I, along with other leaders, had to wade through the time-consuming and frustrating journey with

Glenn as he grew. We had to coach him through his ambition and help him develop the discipline to back it up. He responded with humility every time someone confronted him, and ultimately, this allowed him to continue the journey.

And don't forget: Glenn wrote some amazing songs during this season of his life. He wrote songs that people all around the nation began singing. *Jesus used him.* He was learning and leading worship at New Life at the same time. Some people didn't like it because they thought he was too young, too inexperienced, or too aggressive. But it was worth the effort to allow the Lord to work deeply in his life and ministry. Glenn was anointed and talented; he just needed the right environment for growth.

Mentoring and leading the next generation of young leaders is not pretty. It is messy and difficult, even frustrating at times. But it is worth it! It's worth watching them work and mature, and then find the beauty of a surrendered life that allows them to do the work of the ministry. Raising kids always creates a mess, requires hard work, and calls for a sharp mind. As we commit to the process, having a big family means that there will always be risks and rewards.

RISKS AND REWARDS

Many pastors have trouble taking risks on young leaders with the twenty-first-century American mind-set that the look of success is the way we attract customers. And let's face it: the Sunday-morning service is not where you want to take the most risks. But it must be said one more time—attracting customers is not the same as growing a family or building the kingdom of God. Taking risks on young leaders is something that Jesus did, but He chose intentionally. He spent time with them and included them in the ministry He did. They watched Him heal a sick woman in the middle of a crowd. They observed His propensity to disappear into the trees for prayer. They saw Him touch the leper and be moved with compassion for the people. They listened to Him tell stories to the masses and then really heard Him later when He explained the parables to them. He challenged them, corrected them, encouraged them, and then He finally sent them out on their own, two by two.

If we want to raise up leaders, we must include them and let them see us in our weaknesses and struggles as well as in our successful moments. We've got to let them hang around, ask questions, dialogue with us about what's happening, and give them a behind-the-scenes look at who we are as leaders.

Jesus was just such a leader. He modeled His philosophy in front of His young disciples by eating with tax collectors and sinners. He wasn't the leader who was closed off from the public or from His disciples. He didn't just show up to teach and then disappear behind the curtain. He walked through the crowds with His disciples, stopping along the way to heal, instruct, challenge, and feed.

Jesus established a leadership culture with His disciples and used a leadership method reflected in a well-known chart:

LEADER		FOLLOWER
Do		Watch
Do		Help
Help		Do
Watch		Do

Recently, I spoke to a group of pastors about their relationships with their worship leaders, and I remember the challenge that I issued in answer to a question about how to work with young creative types. I told this room full of older leaders that it was not realistic to hire a twenty-eight-year-old and expect him to know everything that a fifty-year-old would know from experience. In a moment of unexpected intensity, I told them, "Don't hire that talented twenty-eight-year-old musician unless you are willing to spend the time and the energy that is required to develop him into the leader you want him to be. Don't just hire talent and throw them out there on the stage to produce for you!"

I got a few "Amens" and a lot of strange looks.

We should take the risk on the twenty-eight-year-old worship leader, but plan for the mistakes, the coaching, and the failures that will inevitably come. The risk is worth the reward!

INNOVATIVE AND CREATIVE

A common problem with the learning-while-leading paradigm is that most of the next generation wants to take risks creatively. They want to look at issues we face in new ways, and they rarely use the old paradigms. This is what David did when he rejected the armor of Saul and utilized a little-known giant-killing instrument called a sling. One smooth stone (although he had five just in case) was all he needed to fell Goliath. Nobody thought it was possible. No one had even thought about the only space on a giant not covered by armor—his forehead. David innovated and got a zero vote of confidence from his older brothers and King Saul. Allowing young leaders to learn while leading requires us to realize our *need* for their new way of looking at problems. Hopefully, it's not without help, encouragement, and a safety net.

I remember being thirty-four years old and feeling like I was losing it musically. My creativity wasn't what it should have been, and I felt stagnated in my leadership. I knew I needed to recruit more young people to help infuse musical creativity into our ministry. I had breakfast with Jared Anderson, who was home for the winter break from college. He was in his last year and wrestling with what to do after graduation. I wanted him to come back to New Life and spend a couple of years building a foundation before he went out to seek fame and fortune in the secular music business. I told him that I needed him to come and inject some innovation and creativity into our worship. This was before the songwriting culture was created. I just knew I didn't want us to grow stale.

Jared didn't really want to be a worship leader. He had grown up at New Life. His parents were elders. I remember many Saturday-night prayer meetings with Jared playing the piano and singing while we walked around in the auditorium and prayed. He had been raised up in the worship ministry, playing the piano for the youth worship band, and while he definitely loved and appreciated our worship team, he didn't necessarily want to be us.

As it turned out, he felt the Lord leading him to come back and work with us at New Life for one year. Ten years later and the rest is history—powerful songs like "Rescue," "Amazed," "Hear Us from Heaven," "Counting on God," "Be Glorified," and "Great I Am," all written by Jared, are sung in churches around the world. Jared's best days as a songwriter, musician, and author are still ahead, but this ministry through music never would have happened if we hadn't embraced the need for creativity. We have to find ways to allow the innovative and creative spark that lives within the next generation to light up the ministries of our churches.

One lesson I learned in this process came alive to me when I kept hearing from other worship pastors around the country as I taught conferences and seminars. I would tell our story of struggle and success, and they would respond with their own tales of misunderstanding, fear, frustration, and failure in reaching out to the young people in their ministry. "When I try to correct or coach them," these pastors would say, "they just react and pull back, and finally we lose them."

And then it hit me. All of the guys I really invested in and treated as younger brothers, challenging and instructing them, were raised by good parents. They had fathers who loved their mothers. They had moms who loved them and disciplined them. Their fathers raised them with strong training and encouragement as they developed into young men. In a word: *family*. They were each part of a healthy family with a good dad.

Many of these worship pastors or senior pastors were working with young men who didn't have good relationships with their fathers. They weren't raised with a strong hand and a loving embrace. Instead, they had experienced loss, disappointment, or abuse. Their souls were fractured by their family experience, and they had no reference point for healthy feedback, correction, or discipline. The insecurity of a generation raised in a divorce culture has taken a toll on our ability to invest in the next leaders of our churches. The worship pastor at ONEchapel is just such a leader.

PATIENCE AND PERSISTENCE

Marty and his wife, Casey, had come to visit us during the "launch team" phase of our church-planting process. There was still much to be done. They had spent the last year volunteering and serving at New Life Church in Colorado Springs as a result of their own life transition. They were trying to figure out what was next for them. Marty and Casey are both incredibly talented and had great leadership experience. I wondered if God was setting it up for them to come to Austin. We had met only one year earlier, but I really liked them and believed in what God could do in their lives and through them at ONEchapel. We had spoken with them on a couple of occasions about the idea, but with no clear direction. So, after praying about it that night, I asked them to pray about coming to help us.

Three days later, they had leased an apartment in Austin. They heard God speak to them and were quick to obey. This move came with no assurance of salary and a huge leap of faith, for sure, but Marty is nothing if not decisive.

The problems showed up three months later. The hard work of laying the church's foundation and the fear of failure started to cause Marty to panic. Marty is not lazy. He has a strong work ethic, but he also has a strong will. This led him through some pretty serious rebellion as a teenager and still had him convinced that he could do whatever he wanted, and now he wanted to leave. There were too many unknowns with ONEchapel, and that caused him to make a way out.

You see, Marty spent most of his childhood without a father's influence and discipline, which caused him to adopt a bit of an orphan mind-set. With many orphans, the feeling of being alone convinces them that they have no advocate, and that they have to protect themselves because no one else will. It leaves orphans with scars that come from the experience of learning how to fend for themselves; to get what they need and to take what they want. These scars are not always detectable from the outside, but they were driving Marty's fears. I was aware of his past but also believed he was still young enough to be moldable. I thought he was more than worth the risk. He finally told me, "I've realized this isn't for me long term. God did call us to come here to help you launch the church, but now I need to go back and do what I think I'm good at."

My heart sank. I knew the team would be devastated and the church would have to go through the pains of transition—way too soon for our first ex–team member. But I also knew that I could not control it and that there was a process going on inside of Marty—a process that God was in. After a long talk with Aimee and me, Marty and Casey were ready to take a road trip to see if their next move was back to Colorado. At that point, I clearly and respectfully challenged them to evaluate why they were thinking this way and that in my opinion God wouldn't call them to come and help us for just a few short months.

I asked them tons of questions. Was there something deeper? Were they scared or worried? Had I done something to discourage them unknowingly? They wouldn't break. Marty was very matter-of-fact with their decision, and these questions I had would go unanswered. I wanted to jump up and down and scream, "You're crazy! This is nuts! Don't do it! Can't you see how much potential there is here? Don't you believe in this vision?" But I didn't. I just communicated that my life calling as a pastor is to encourage what

Jesus is doing in the lives of others. If they didn't want to be here for whatever reason, then I was for helping them take their next step into what God had for them. I told them to come back next week and let me know what the next step was. That night, I remember being on the front porch of our house where I felt prompted to say, "I can see you're wrestling. If this isn't the right direction for you, come back and let me help you figure it out. I'm for you."

That was really hard to do. I closed the door and turned to my wife. "Well, it's over. The only way they'll be able to come back to ONEchapel is if they return with tears in their eyes telling us that they were crazy and that they don't know what they were thinking." Don't get me wrong. I was still willing to help them figure out where to go next, but I'd seen enough of these situations to know that when team members want to leave, you don't typically try to stop them. But still, I had this sneaking suspicion that God was doing something and that I should be patient.

A week later, my suspicions were confirmed. We, once again, had them over to our house and began to talk. Marty had utilized the past week to prearrange everything to return to Colorado—working with the School of Worship, teaching private lessons, and serving in the worship ministry at New Life. He had even left his car in Colorado, expecting to return. But the conversation took a very personal and intimate turn. Rather than seeking to convince me that the move back to Colorado was best, he began to confess his fears and share his deepest insecurities. Through tears, he began to let me know that he just wanted to escape. He was worried that he wouldn't be able to do what I was asking him to do, that ultimately he would fail and lose control. Life would be easier if he just returned to doing something he knew he could do. Too much responsibility and too many unknowns had taken over. These were his greatest fears.

Marty repented of resisting the voice of God telling him to stay the course at ONEchapel—almost a "Jonah-like" experience, according to him. He explained how rebellion had been a way of life for him and how he'd always been able to do whatever he wanted. He'd never been in a situation where a father figure or pastor would patiently walk through this kind of process with him. He'd never felt truly safe to speak of this orphan mind-set that he had lived by for so long. It was a breakthrough in his life. Casey watched him pour his heart out, and she helped fill in the blanks as we zeroed in on this long-standing stronghold in his life to control everything around him and become vulnerable to no one. It was a miracle happening before our eyes.

We've never looked back. God may call Marty to go on to another place of ministry at some point, but it definitely won't be any time soon. He and Casey have purchased a house here in Austin and are pregnant with their first baby. He's thirty-one years old now and becoming the man God wants him to be. He's a great leader, and he's learning and growing by leaps and bounds. He's surely not perfect, but no one is. Marty is called and anointed to pastor others, and our relationship is more secure than ever. He's more secure than ever. He and Casey have found a home. They know they belong to the ONEchapel family.

The lesson is in the process. Most pastors would have cut them loose right at the moment that he said this wasn't the place for him. This "if you're not with us you're against us" attitude permeates the institutional church generation that came before us. For some, there is zero tolerance for this kind of processing and doubt in the life of a young leader. There are way too many stories of young pastors or leaders being cut off from their church as soon as they express any doubt, concern, or anxiety about their future. Often, senior leaders don't allow for them to openly wrestle through fears and settle insecurities. They don't take time, and they typically don't have the patience.

Pastors can easily get focused on the job instead of the people. In a church, the people are the point of everything we're doing, and that truth should hold firm for our staff, leaders, and team members. It's the only way we keep the whole church healthy. If we let the ministry machine chew up our people and spit them out, wounded, hurt, and cynical, we've destroyed the very reason we exist—to liberate people's potential, to see them empowered, equipped, cared for, loved, and doing what God designed them to do.

In this next generation coming up, we're going to have to lovingly and patiently teach them the truth through a process that may take a little longer than it used to. The fear and insecurity of a divorce culture have stunted the growth of our twentysomethings. We're going to have to teach them how to live in a healthy family. We've got to model it and provide security and stability for them as they grow. We're going to have to train them to trust and show them that it's safe to process with a person in authority without risking their livelihood. We're going to have to repair the damage and watch the miracle unfold as God re-creates the family in our churches. We need mentors, fathers, mothers, older brothers and sisters who will teach the next generation that they are accepted and loved even in the midst of conflict, correction, and challenge.

It is possible because God is a healer.

But it's going to take more energy, effort, and time. Don't be afraid of it; just realize that you will have to lay a foundation of love for their lives before you start building their ministry skills and shaping their gifts.

Very often the process takes a toll on an older generation, which lives by a different set of values. There is always a struggle to integrate young and old together. Families can be challenging. It can be intimidating for an older generation to deal with their own insecurities as mentors, but as the talent in the next generation becomes obvious and once both young and old alike embrace humility, we can learn how to work together. And make no mistake; it takes time, energy, risks, and several servings of humble pie for us all to become a family—brothers, sisters, comrades, and friends.

HUMILITY AND HONOR

I have never been perfect in the implementation of this multi-generational ministry model. I've made mistakes. I controlled too much sometimes and was too hands off at other times. I was insecure one moment and overconfident at others.

The secret for me was to embrace a culture of humility and honor so that no matter our successes or failures, we always had the opportunity to learn from them. It is this atmosphere cultivated by a mature and steady hand that allows young people to grow into leadership. Look at what 1 Peter 5:1–7 says to us who are elders and shepherds over those who are younger:

> To the elders among you, I appeal as a fellow elder
> and a witness of Christ's sufferings who also will

share in the glory to be revealed: Be shepherds of God's flock that is under your care, watching over them—not because you must, but because you are willing, as God wants you to be; not pursuing dishonest gain, but eager to serve; not lording it over those entrusted to you, but being examples to the flock. And when the Chief Shepherd appears, you will receive the crown of glory that will never fade away.

In the same way, you who are younger, submit yourselves to your elders. All of you, clothe yourselves with humility toward one another, because, "God opposes the proud but shows favor to the humble."

Humble yourselves, therefore, under God's mighty hand, that he may lift you up in due time. Cast all your anxiety on him because he cares for you.

Verse 3 begins the meddling. Authority isn't for lording over but for providing examples. Notice how verse 5 encourages young people to submit to elders, but then in the next breath, Peter said, "All of you, clothe yourselves with humility."

Humility isn't as much a character trait as an action. We must clothe ourselves with it. We choose to wear it or we don't. If God has to humble us, it's too late—and that's going to be a bad day. We all have to demonstrate the humility of Christ in our actions.

If we are corrected, we respond with openheartedness and grace. If we are mistreated, we respond in maturity and kindness. If we make a mistake, we admit it, apologize sincerely, and move forward.

If we are irritated at the incredibly brilliant young mind challenging us, we maintain an attitude of humility and use speech that may be firm but seasoned with grace.

These are the marks of humility.

Why would we do this? Because God opposes the proud and favors the humble! One thing is for sure: I do not want to be opposed by God. In fact, I'm absolutely sure that I cannot do what He's called me to do without His favor and faithfulness in my life.

It doesn't matter if you are young or old as you read this, the admonition is for all of us to wear humility like a garment of clothing. This passage ends with a final nod to those who are bent on ambition—typically the young among us. The instruction is simple: humble yourselves so that God can lift you up in due time. His timeline is better than yours. Take your time. Be faithful, humble, and consistent, and don't worry about how fast you rise in your career or ministry. Cast your anxiety about all of this on Him, and have confidence that He knows and cares about you.

Look at how the apostle Paul shared this idea with Timothy, his young son in the faith:

> Do not rebuke an older man harshly, but exhort him
> as if he were your father. Treat younger men as broth-
> ers, older women as mothers, and younger women as
> sisters, with absolute purity. (1 Tim. 5:1–2)

There's no better description for how a family should live together, allowing each other to make mistakes, learn lessons, and grow into the mature and influential leaders God called us all to be.

HOW THE UNDER-30S LEAD AND LEARN

One of the challenges of working in a multigenerational context is the variation in cultural norms and values between generations. Perceived work ethics, or lack thereof, technological abilities, and the speed of communication that is generally acceptable to each generation are all part of how the family comes together.

Here are a few considerations:

Multitasking

It is not uncommon for a young person to look down at his or her mobile device and begin texting while listening to someone or engaging in conversation. This practice doesn't seem rude or inconsiderate to them. When I was growing up, my dad taught me that if someone is talking to you, then you look them straight in the eye.

I realize that our cultural values are in flux, but there is no getting around the fact that our young people are uniquely equipped to converse, text, listen to music, surf the web, watch TV, email, and work on a project all at the same time. Just one mobile device facilitates all of this and reinforces the fact that they can and should do it. Multitasking is something our current generation of young people does well, and we must embrace them, while at the same time teaching them acceptable manners. They can do a lot at the same time and in many ways function best when loaded up with multiple tasks.

Technological Integration

Most young people in our culture have grown up with a laptop, mobile phone, gaming device, or an iPod in their hands. Though this often makes them technologically savvy, it also causes them to believe that they can and should be allowed to do things at their own pace and on their own schedule. No longer is work limited to the hours between 9:00 a.m. and 5:00 p.m., and now with telecommuting and working from home becoming common, often their work takes place outside the office. This freedom is taken for granted and sometimes feels to older adults like a poor work ethic or laziness. An older generation put up with difficult conditions while they earned the right to have their own schedule, but this generation is doing things differently. Life and work are all mixed up together as anyone on Facebook can tell you. We're going to have to integrate this virtual workplace into our churches and use it to the best of our ability to connect with people in this technological era.

Both older and younger need to open their minds to compromise on this point. Consider allowing people to work from home or the coffee shop instead of being chained to a desk. Young people also need to be part of the team and at times demonstrate that commitment by being around. Work on the balance of freedom and connectedness to find the most effectiveness in your team.

Speed of Communication

It's common for me to receive a text message from my fifteen-year-old son while I'm at work. He'll call me a short time later and demand an answer to the texted question. Incredulous, he will say, "Didn't you get my text?" Technology has sped up life for all of us, but those who are older are the only ones who seem to have noticed. For the latest generation, Facebook, Skype, Twitter, and phone-texting technology have given them an instantaneous feedback-and-response mechanism that is now part of their social, cultural, and personal development. This is unprecedented freedom that translates into other areas. Younger workers run circles around older workers, and this requires humility on both sides of the table. We all must be willing to work together, deploying our strengths and compensating for each other's weaknesses—and this is the beauty of intergenerational ministry. Older folks, don't be afraid to catch up and learn new technology. Young folks, slow down a little and be helpful to the old-timers.

These are just three examples of some of the challenges that must be overcome between generations, and there are many others. But the next generation doesn't want us to be like them; they want us to be who we are and relate to them as family members. They have a hunger for mentors, coaches, and, yes, fathers and mothers who will love them, accept them, and help them navigate their lives, convincing them that they can be successful leaders in our churches—even while they learn.

Chapter 7

BOTOX BELIEVERS

One of the smartest and funniest coming-of-age movies of the recent past is *Mean Girls*, written by Tina Fey, the ever-popular and witty former star of *Saturday Night Live* and current star of *30 Rock*.

In *Mean Girls* one character has become the stereotypical "cool mom." The mom who wants to be young so badly that she will do anything to portray a hip and trendy image, including dressing inappropriately, using current cultural expressions she has no business using, and allowing her daughter to do pretty much anything she wants. All this the cool mom does in the name of gaining her daughter's acceptance, along with the acceptance of her daughter's goofy friends.

This is a stereotype that continues in our culture and is represented by the Botox-loving, bubble-gum-chewing, gossiping, adolescent image on reality TV shows like *The Housewives of _____* (name the urban city of choice).

Over the years, I have watched the church try to become the "cool mom" to the people of our culture. She dresses funny, talks weird, and seems desperate to be accepted. She makes decisions, not based on what is best for the family, but on what makes her awesome and acceptable in the young eyes of our culture. The struggle to remain relevant has pulled at the church since its inception, but we're tempted now more than ever to be accepted by the world for the sake of influence. Nowhere has this been more pronounced than in the commitment of our churches to reach the next generation.

THE POSTMODERN PHENOMENON

For many years, churches across North America have wrestled with the question of how to reach the next generation. Churches have created programs and pathways for ministering to young people, and youth departments have been a staple of ministry since the 1950s. Churches today wrestle with a deeper concern. The emergent-church discussion within American Christianity signaled a shift in the thinking of many church leaders. Books and seminars sprang up everywhere, telling us that our entire ministries needed to change in the face of this cultural tidal wave. Old systems and structures had to go. Absolutes could not be articulated with the same fervency. Answers should be veiled in relevance to allow this new generation to find out for themselves who God is. Pastors scrambled to make the transition to relevancy with new worship styles, experiential teaching methods, and new paradigms of church ministry. In those years I talked to many worship leaders and pastors who were so confused by those who said, "The sky is falling, and you'd better prepare for the new millennium."

Indeed, the truth is that many of our churches needed to change. The worship wars were mostly over, and few churches fought over whether or not new worship styles should be embraced. Most pastors and churches agreed change was imminent. The fight was now over implementation.

As a result, the last decade has been filled with experimentation. How will we remake our church culture? Today the fight is over an attractional model versus a missional model. I'm not convinced that these models are mutually exclusive. They will most likely converge for most churches, which will try to implement the strengths of both, but there are still questions about how each of these models deals with the question of the generations. We ought not wait too long to decide.

WAITING TOO LONG TO DECIDE

When a church resists change for too long, it finds itself losing the next generation of young people who could continue the vision and vibrancy of the church.

It happens innocently enough. A church develops a liturgy and style comfortable for its attendees. The music, environment, and people join together to create the culture of a church that eventually falls behind the curve of the culture it's trying to reach. It happens slowly and unnoticeably in little decisions and seemingly insignificant emotional attachments—song selections, potlucks, special music, and Saturday-morning men's breakfasts—then all of a sudden they look around, and everybody is talking about empty nests and bodyaches. The young people have gone off to college; young families have taken jobs in other cities, and slowly the church realizes it's not reaching a younger demographic.

This sudden sense of urgency creates two alternatives for churches.

The first response for many church leaders is simply to create a next-generation service with its own culture, style, and liturgy. The rationale for creating an alternative service is simple. The older generation can continue to observe the traditions and enjoy the musical styles of their own service, while the next generation can experiment and try new styles in a service of their own.

No danger of splitting the church wide open with a new worship style.

This is not necessarily a bad solution. It preserves the organization and allows the church to experiment with minimal conflict. It allows the church to widen its influence without taking too much risk. However, the challenge lies in the fact that there will be two distinct and different churches in the congregation. One will grow old and die, while the other will rise up to take its place. Sometimes this takes the form of a church plant. Other times it feels more like a church split. There are churches trying to keep both groups stable long enough to transition them back together, but I don't know of many attempts that have been successful.

The second option for churches is to completely overhaul the worship style and culture of the primary service. Often the pastor moves quickly, and the radical change alienates some and embraces others. People who are unhappy are told this is what we have to do to reach the next generation and that if they don't like it, "Don't let the door hit ya where the good Lord split ya!" This is not the worst thing in the world either, because churches, just like all service organizations, need continual growth and modification to keep them efficient and effective.

Both of these options are normal in churches around our nation, and I'm not suggesting they are entirely wrongheaded or poorly motivated. I don't know of any church that isn't genuinely trying to reach out to the current generation as well as the next.

In fact, years ago at New Life Church, we started a more traditional service as we recognized the changing landscape. We were one of the only churches I knew of that went backward—a contemporary church that needed to offer more traditional elements in worship.

Loads of pastors and churches are still specifically targeting one generation and building their culture around that generation. But it works only for a while, and before you know it, that generation starts having kids.

There is nothing more enjoyable than to watch a young dad wake up to the idea that he is not as "cool" as he once was. I like to call it the "minivan syndrome." You can drive your SUV for only so long before it happens. You need something more convenient, more reliable, safer, and more affordable. The next thing you know, you're test-driving a Dodge Caravan. The desire to be cool gives way to the need for convenience, and suddenly, without warning, you turn around one year and you've become your dad, wearing your black dress socks with tennis shoes.

For me, the question is not about the effectiveness of either one of these models for reaching the next generation. The question is what are we giving up when we choose one or the other. I think there may be a better way. I believe there is a third way, which rejects the consumer-driven model and embraces a family model that prioritizes belonging.

But first a brief lesson in modern church history.

THE SEEDS OF A CONSUMER CHURCH

I first heard the term "generation X" when I was in college. We were the generation they couldn't figure out, and it was said we reacted to the cause-driven nature of our parents. We followed the baby boomers, so to some we were baby busters! Some of us talked about doing church "our way," or in ways it had never been done before. The way it should be done! In a word: *relevant*.

Gen-X services began to spring up everywhere. Of course, we were not the first to try to reflect current culture, rejecting the rigidity of Christian traditions. The Christian tradition is filled with people trying to do church better and more like the early church. In the '70s though, the established mainline denominations dismissed some boomers as long-haired hippies, but with their massive population numbers, they began to dominate the cultural landscape.

The '60s and '70s were decades of great societal upheaval in America. Civil rights, women's rights, government corruption, the Vietnam War, the threat of communism, and the Cold War challenged the authoritarian social structures that had held the proverbial keys to the car in twentieth-century America. But the upheaval of these decades came from the fact that this was the first time the majority of the American population was under thirty years old. Idealistic and enthusiastic teenagers and twentysomethings began to influence and eventually shape every sphere of culture and society.

As the largest population demographic to pass through American society, boomers began to dominate everything from fashion to politics. Their influence and distrust of anyone over thirty years old could be felt in art, government, academics, housing, finance, and, yes, the marketplace, as they wielded massive purchasing power. Ad executives began to target this demographic group, and niche marketing was born (or maybe grew up). The fourteen-to-thirty-four age demographic is now an entrenched market staple of TV, movies, fashion, music, and more as a result.

The seeds of this niche-marketing concept ultimately found their way into the church and grew into what we now call a consumer model of church. The creation of generational church services and specialized experiences for different age-groups exploded into the megachurch movement of the 1980s and '90s. Young leaders responded to the rejection of mainline churches by devising their own "brand" and found new ways of doing church.

The so-called Jesus People hungered for authenticity and a genuine demonstration of God's power. They ended up using their cause-driven mind-set and context to create their own church culture, unencumbered by traditions. Incredibly, history may be repeating today.

I maintain that the American church should always embrace the process of reinventing itself culturally, even while the message remains the same. It's part of our rugged American individualism and our free-market-driven society. Every new generation that comes along thinks it is the first one to have these thoughts. Young people are experiencing so many new ideas and formulating their own view of the world, making it quite natural for them to get lost in an ideology that they think is new. It takes a little time and experience before they realize they're just the latest ones to join their voices with many who desire genuine and authentic relationships. My big question is, Can we aid in this generational-discovery process and encourage their questioning without fearing a loss of control or relevance?

The question is, Can we keep this cycle of rejecting the old and promoting the new from destroying our churches? Is it possible to reject the paradigm of consumer-driven church and replace it with something more holistic and multigenerational?

Can we close the perceived generation gaps and do life together?

My question for all the older leaders of large churches is simple. Will you include the next generation? Not for the sake of mere survival or cultural relevance, but because you want to perpetuate the work of the kingdom of God and transfer your wisdom, experience, and resources to the next generation. I fear that many older leaders may not be able to let go of the scepter of these massive ministries they've built to "connect the next generation." Most young leaders are having to build something on their own in the church instead of transitioning an already-mature ministry. Again, this is not necessarily bad, but what have we given up? Are these young leaders having to learn the harsh lessons of church life and ministry all over again without the wisdom of their mentors?

Is it surprising that in the midst of the last twenty years, after we've been inundated with leadership, worship ministry and church-planting materials, resources, books, and conferences, that our own corporate church services seem more shallow and performance driven than ever? Not if you realize that we've just been feeding the monster of church growth and strategy rather than building a family. You see, the answer to our depth and relevance as a church is not just about the content of our church services. It is actually about the personnel who lead our church services.

This is the great challenge of our consumer-driven church culture. We can choose any number of these twenty-first-century ways to build our churches, but at what cost? What will we give up if we surrender to the two great idols of our American church culture, choice and convenience? Instead of offering a family of diverse people and interests, we offer homogenous services produced to meet our individual demands. Instead of teaching self-sacrifice and love, we make church about our expediency, ease, and comfort. Suddenly, we'll be surrounded by our own kind—old and grumpy—with no one to share our experience, wisdom, and resources with. We just spend it all on ourselves, not realizing that we're starting to become obsolete.

"A PIRATE LOOKS AT FORTY"

I remember the first time it happened to me. I was thirty-six years old and didn't realize what was going on. I had agreed to play flag football with a bunch of college-age students in an annual tournament at New Life Church that we called "The Ice Bowl." Held in November every year, the event had grown to multiple brackets over two days when teams would slug it out on the gridiron for the championship.

I don't know if you realize this or not, but everyone who has ever played flag football knows that flag football is not really flag football.

It's tackle football with flags.

There were no pads, but depending on our Colorado temperatures people often wore as many layers of clothing as they could fit into. Plus, this particular tournament attracted sports enthusiasts from all over the region, and the teams often recruited big, hairy, and muscled men from places like the Air Force Academy to play.

So this was tough, bloody, hard-core flag football!

I played quarterback for our team from the New Life School of Worship (stop laughing). We won the first game in our bracket, lost the next game, and finally were ousted after our second loss in the double-elimination tournament.

The next morning, I got up out of bed feeling incredible soreness all over my body. My muscles weren't just aching; they were screaming with deep soreness that wouldn't end. I hobbled around for a day or two thinking that I had just overdone it, but the pain just wouldn't go away. After five days, I knew something was wrong.

I called my father-in-law, who is an ER doctor, and told him all of my symptoms. I said, "Something has got to be wrong with me." He listened carefully and probed with some questions about my body and medical history, and then he said, "Well, I've got good news and bad news for you."

"What's the good news?" I replied.

He said, "You're going to be just fine."

"And the bad news?" I retorted.

"You're just getting old," he responded.

I yelled with disbelief, "You've got to be kidding me! This can't be what it feels like to get old."

And this was his response: "Oh no, it gets worse!"

This was my first look into the mirror of mortality. My body showed its first signs of aging, and it was utterly discouraging. I realized that I was losing something, and part of me had begun to wear out. It gave me that feeling of loss and a certain sense of panic at the thought of running out of time. Like the Jimmy Buffett song "A Pirate Looks at Forty," I wanted to hold on to my youth, fearful of running out of time. But of course, we're all helpless in fending off the subtle effects of growing older.

GROWING THE CHURCH YOUNGER

Churches often feel this way. They want to hold on to what they've got and fend off the effects of aging, but it's the wrong thing to do. Instead, we've got to gently open our hands to the next generation and pass on whatever God has placed in our hands.

There is a sentence that perfectly describes the challenge facing every single church that desires to become multigenerational. This sentence is not tricky or exceptionally brilliant, but it is profound. It is a simple truth that cuts to the core of where we must put our energy and effort as a family church.

Study it. Meditate on it. Memorize it!

Here it is:

It takes no skill or expertise for a church to grow older.

I know. I built it up too much, didn't I?

But it's true. We don't really have to work at growing the church older because it happens *naturally*. It happens *automatically*. People work together and live life together, and they grow old. All the hard work for a church is in continually reaching down to the next generation and including them in the life of the family.

I believe healthy churches grow just like healthy families. When my children's grandparents see my two oldest boys, who are ages seventeen and fifteen, they always say, "My, how you have grown! I can hardly believe how big you are!" They have never once followed it by asking me this question: "How are you doing that?"

The challenge for every community of believers is to make sure that through the years they are continually inviting the next generation of leaders to step up and really lead. The church actively grows younger by supporting and pushing young people. This is an essential paradigm for healthy families, and it reveals itself in every church as well. Parents often have trouble allowing their children to grow up into adults and transitioning from a parent-child relationship to a counselor-friend relationship. The age difference will always be there, but many parents have trouble seeing their children as mature, and frankly, kids have a difficult journey in realizing that their parents should become their friends and counselors.

Churches are subject to this same challenge. They often don't allow the young to genuinely engage in the life-giving and messy ministry of the church in a meaningful way. They keep them in perpetual training. They cling to their long-held positions of significance for far too long. They fear that they will become irrelevant.

As the baby boomers age, the question is, Will they allow the next generation to lead *with* them, or will they force the next generation to start their own ministries without the accountability, resources, love, and wisdom of their own experience? Will they separate the young from the old, or will they choose to wrestle with a multigenerational and messy third way? Will they actually invite them to have a place at the table of church ministry and leadership?

MY TEST OF MATURITY

As a young man who was having success in leading worship at New Life Church, I remember the fear that gripped me as I began to mentor and encourage younger worship leaders. I recruited Glenn Packiam from Oral Roberts University, my alma mater, because my youngest brother had been his roommate for a year. I met Glenn as he passed through Colorado Springs five years earlier with some friends. He had played the piano and sung me a song that he had written, leaving a worship demo of new songs with me.

Five years later he was the assistant director of music ministries at ORU, and I was trying to convince him to come apprentice with me at New Life. It was certainly a step down for him. But, in a sign of humility and sensitivity to the voice of the Holy Spirit, he came to work with me and lay the groundwork for starting a school of worship. Jared Anderson came next. His parents were elders in our church, and I asked him to come back and help us for a year before he followed his dreams of becoming a full-time musician. Jon Egan had never written a song before he came to New Life. He came to lead worship for my brother Brent, who was the youth pastor at New Life at that time. They were best friends who had gone to school together.

All three of these talented young men came to our church with ideas, vision, dreams, and hopes for ministry. They began to grow musically, relationally, and pastorally. Another young man, named David Perkins, came to New Life, and he wanted to begin a youth conference called Desperation. We held the first Desperation Conference in the World Prayer Center with no more than a few hundred kids. It was raw, innocent, and passionate, and we felt God was building something.

Glenn, Jared, and Jon had all been writing songs along with others, and Integrity Music was publishing our songs and recording projects. I had already recorded "Lord of the Harvest" and "Around Your Throne," and together we geared up for more. It was a time of experimenting and stretching, and we all enjoyed the fruit of what God was doing among us in our church. It made sense that these three young men would lead worship for the Desperation Conference and write some music for it.

But then something happened.

Integrity decided that it would publish the Desperation project with its very own CD release. More songs were written. The project released and the Desperation Band was born.

Suddenly, this band of upstarts was doing their own thing, and people really liked it. *Could this be a threat to my success?* I wondered.

The students appeared to surpass the teacher, and honestly, that was really disconcerting to me at the time. I had to make a fundamental decision about the successes of these young men. Would I be willing to promote, encourage, and celebrate their success even to the detriment of my own?

Of course, there was plenty of room for all to succeed, but it didn't feel like it to me then. There are only a certain number of songs that can go on a CD, and most of their songs were better than my songs!

In that season I wrestled with my own insecurity. I faced my fears of failure and loss. I prayed a lot. I decided that God's plan for me was good enough, and that I could encourage God's good plans for others, even above my own desires. I realized that God's work in me was enough and that His desires for me were the only thing that mattered. I needed to work hard, challenge myself, and encourage the success of all of the other young men and women who were coming up behind me.

With God's grace, I realized that my job might be to promote and support others who were going to be more successful at what I wanted to do. I concluded that I could never stand in the way of what God wanted to do with others, and why would I want to? And that's when the transition happened.

I began to enjoy the process of mentoring and encouraging the growth of these young leaders more than ever. I started reveling in their success! I felt the deep satisfaction of creating a platform for them and the fulfillment of partnership and accomplishment. I rejoiced in their development and began to see the kingdom purpose in us all. We were, and are still, friends. I consider them to be peers now more than ever, but my transition from a competitor to a coach and from a brother's rival to a father's heart was invaluable to all of our success.

This is the challenge of every middle-aged person who wants success and significance through raising up the next generation. The lesson here is that our own significance often comes more through the empowerment and success of others than through the work of our own hands. When we're willing to encourage God's work in others and love them like He does, we find His purpose and impact in our own lives. We become successful by making others successful.

This was a great discovery in my life, but in reality, I was just repeating what had been done for me by others.

MY PLACE IN THE FAMILY

I was a "young" twenty-five-year-old college student when Ted Haggard met me and invited me to consider moving to Colorado Springs to help continue to build a thriving congregation of fifteen hundred by leading worship at New Life Church. I took the job and ended up helping the youth pastor, Chris Hodges, work with kids on Wednesday nights, and leading worship on Sundays. It was a great time of learning and growing for me. Ted was ten years older than I was, and our work together created a philosophy of ministry that continues to shape my view of multigenerational church to this day.

The "twenty-year influence gap" is essentially the view that each leader has an influence range with people who are ten years ahead of him or her and ten years behind him or her. The idea is that every senior pastor has a primary influence range of about twenty years. When I came to work at New Life, at twenty-five, I was ten years younger than the senior pastor. Based on this theory, my influence range was for people ages fifteen to thirty-five. Today, I pastor ONEchapel in Austin, Texas, and I am forty-five years old. That means that I should have a primary influence range of about thirty-five to fifty-five.

Now, I like to say I get to cheat younger because I look so young and vibrant! Some say that I also have a younger style of communicating. But I think pastors who think multigenerationally expand their influence toward the next generation if they continue to stay up-to-date with culture. I'm not talking about the backward hat and goatee that personified the youth pastor of the '90s. Nor am I recommending some kind of fashion statement with the trendy, elaborately stitched shirts of the 2000s that became some pastors' dress codes. Cool glasses, printed T-shirts, aggressive worship music, and many references to "the millennials" can actually make a pastor more irrelevant. What do we say about a fifty-year-old who tries to dress like a twenty-five-year-old? We say he's having a midlife crisis.

In my experience, twenty-five-year-olds want fifty-year-olds to act their age. They don't want them to try to be overly hip or relevant. They want their wisdom. They want their love, help, and protection. At age forty-five, I've realized the boundaries of my "coolness" and instead embraced the value that I can bring to the next generation. Teaching, training, experience, encouragement, and resources are the contributions that I can make to the hearts of the next leaders of our church.

I think ONEchapel, the church I lead today, is an "emerging church" and will be for the next twenty years. New Life Church, where I spent over eighteen years, was probably always an emerging church. However, I think the title is a misnomer. New Life continued to emerge with different cultural elements because we kept evolving. The family kept growing up. We kept changing to meet the demands of our culture. We kept embracing the next generation, and that transformed our church culture. The message never changed, but we overhauled our methods many times.

I've embraced a philosophy that will guide our church through transitions and changes for years to come. I believe we need to embrace what God is doing and participate with what is happening in the body of Christ now, but not get stuck in one fad or another. At ONEchapel we build on Bible teaching and worship. It's not a platform-driven church. The ministry doesn't begin and end with the pastoral staff and the pastor's teaching (thank God!). We want people to connect and relate. We want their ideas and gifts to drive ministry, to be innovative, and to come up with concepts that we never would have thought of on our own. We're going to maintain our steadiness in ministry through the seasons and different emphases within the larger church. We'll always be a family church with a strong multi-generational culture. We don't have to be something we're not. In years to come we can take on the look of a church that is settled with itself, a church with a rich heritage, but a family of believers that is engaged in what God is doing in this generation and the ones to come.

FLESH-AND-BONE CHURCH

Botox synthetically reduces the wrinkles earned after many years of experience. It injects something unnatural and dangerous into the face or other body parts. Botox represents the desire to stay young at all costs—to be obsessed with appearance rather than wisdom. The bubble-gum-smacking, expressionless "cool-mom" church is only a facade. People hunger for a more authentic church that will not be consumed with perfectly programmed services and spiritual fast food with little or no nutritional value. Rather, they want a church with smudges and rough edges that's not afraid to express and feel the difficult emotions of a real and sometimes altogether messy family!

If you're an older person with lines starting to form around your eyes, don't be ashamed. Mentor someone instead. If you're a singer whose voice isn't quite as elastic and pretty as it once was, don't grip the microphone even tighter. Open your heart to a new role and share. If your hair is graying a bit, don't feel like you have to go out and buy the latest hair-color product. Be willing to accept who you are and realize that there are young people who need your experience.

They need your wisdom.

They need your coaching.

And they especially need your love.

Chapter 8

LOVE MAKES A HOUSE A HOME

When we planted ONEchapel in Austin, Texas, in September 2010, I had one major goal: to build a real church. I didn't want to build a corporate entity with spiritual duties. I didn't want to create a social organization simply to do good things; I wanted to invest in a real, authentic, flesh-and-bone church full of people who loved each other deeply and cared for each other's needs.

As I sit writing these words, I have tremendous confidence that we are well on our way. People are sharing their lives with one another and serving each other in a way that demonstrates our love for Christ.

Last year, we had our first Memorial Day Weekend Picnic, Baptism, and Night of Worship under a big tent near our church offices. It was incredible to watch five hundred people breaking bread together, talking, laughing, praying for each other, and becoming a genuine family. What you would notice is that these people are an eclectic bunch. We have former gang members with tattoos, silver-haired business owners, twentysomething college students, middle-aged parents with kids, Democrats, Republicans, independents, Hispanics, African Americans, Dallas Cowboy fans, and Pittsburgh Steeler fans—all learning how to surrender their rights and identifying marks to take up the mark of Christ.

It is a miracle!

Love is always a miracle. God's love for us transforms our lives. Our love for one another comes as a result. If there is one thing that our churches should be known for, it is love—Jesus said as much when He told His disciples in John 13:35 that they would be recognized by their love for each other. There is no greater love than to lay down our lives for each other, and that especially includes those who are different from us. In fact, we are living answers to the prayer of Jesus. *Yes.* The prayers Jesus Christ, God's one and only Son, prayed to the Father in John 17. It was this very prayer of His that started me down the road of dreaming what our church should be.

Look at what Jesus said in His prayer:

> My prayer is not for them alone. I pray also for those who will believe in me through their message, that all of them may be one, Father, just as you are in me and I am in you. May they also be in us so that the world may believe that you have sent me. I have given them the glory that you gave me, that they may be one as we are one—I in them and you in me—so that they may be brought to complete unity. Then the world will know that you sent me and have loved them even as you have loved me. (John 17:20–23)

Jesus prayed that we would have the kind of love and unity that the world would see and, as a result, discover Him. Jesus's prayer is to make us into a people who understand our identity as well as Jesus knew His own. When we understand who we are, love easily flows from us and reveals Jesus. His prayer to His Father was that we would be willing to give up our own identifying marks as individuals—race, gender, class, etc.—and take on the mark of Christ. Then we embrace being known as Christians, God's children, and our identity is found in His family rather than in our own interests, rights, or experiences. Taking on the identity of Christ is a significant concept that helps define who we are as God's people. Out of many, we become *one*! That is the power of Jesus's prayer and also the theme behind ONEchapel. We are not divided by our individualism; instead, we surrender to loving one another and living in harmony and unity.

The amazing part of this prayer is that Jesus wants us to realize that the Father loves us the same way He loves Jesus. He loves us just as much as He loves His own Son—the firstborn among many brothers and sisters (Rom. 8:29). This is the love of the family of God. This love is a distinguishing mark for our church and makes us unique in the world!

LOVING PEOPLE WHO ARE NOT LIKE US (THE GENERATIONAL CHALLENGE)

Imagine an ice-cream joint that sells only one flavor of ice cream. It serves vanilla. No rocky road, cookies and cream, or mint chocolate chip. Just vanilla. Not thirty-one flavors, not even two flavors that you might swirl together, making your eyes sparkle as you await that first lick. That ice-cream shop will be boring, one dimensional, and out of business soon enough.

A similar thing happens in many of our churches. Homogenous churches are the most natural and automatic tendency we have as the American church. Scott Williams, the author of *Church Diversity,* cites a *Time* article reporting that 93 percent of our churches are racially segregated.[1] We live in the land of freedom, where we can peaceably assemble with anyone we'd like, and we are free to enjoy the company of whomever we choose. But there's one thing wrong with this way of thinking. It's not biblical!

The Bible teaches us that we aren't allowed to pass through our lives spending time with people of our own choosing for our own enjoyment. We cannot stay cloistered inside of our own churches, befriending people with whom we have so much in common. We must cross cultural barriers and break through walls of prejudice. We must love those who are our enemies, pray for those who mistreat us, and lay our lives down for one another (Luke 6:27–28).

In Matthew 28:18–20, one last time before He left the earth and returned to heaven, Jesus highlighted our responsibility to love people who are different from us. In this passage, He charged His disciples to go and make more disciples in all nations. In Acts 1:8 He encouraged His disciples to wait and receive the power that made them witnesses in Jerusalem, and in all Judea and Samaria, and to the ends of the earth. Here Jesus described three types of people to whom we should witness: people like us who have the same culture, those who are just outside of our comfort zone, and finally the people who have no common cultural or societal connection to us. We're called to share with them all. In fact, Jesus said these words to people who really did not like the people of Samaria. They would have heard His words the same way a die-hard, right-wing, southern Republican Christian would hear instructions to share Christ's love with a liberal, intellectual, northern Democrat atheist. We're not called to love just our own people. Missionary work is not for a select few; it is necessary for all of us who want to follow Christ.

We must be willing to lay down our lives for people who are not like us. In fact, it is the best and most powerful expression of the gospel when we lay our lives down for those who think, speak, and act completely different from us. It is this kind of laying-your-life-down love that should characterize Christians.

What are we missing when we separate the generations in church? We're missing the centerpiece of the gospel message: *love*. We're missing the key ingredient of laying down our lives for another.

Jesus made His most convincing argument for this kind of love when He told the story of the "Good Samaritan." This is the quintessential picture of embracing the cultural challenges of reaching out to someone in need who is not like you.

In Luke 10, Jesus told this story as a response to the question "Who is my neighbor?" It is clear from the passage that an expert in the law was trying to define very carefully whom he was responsible to love. In essence, he wanted to qualify some people as nonneighbors and discover whom he did not have to love.

Jesus told the story in a way that may have surprised all those listening. The road from Jerusalem to Jericho was a stretch of road well known for danger and criminal activity. Jesus began with a well-respected priest who passed by a bloody and beaten traveler. A revered Levite passed by next, but he avoided the helpless man in the ditch and passed without the least bit of notice. Jesus knew the crowds would be guessing who came next. Most likely they'd be ready for Him to say that a Pharisee passed by and helped the man. Pharisees were the most sacred protectors of the Torah. They were separatists whose ceremonial purity was regarded as holiness in that culture. In fact, the very word *Pharisee* means "separated." It would have made sense to the Jewish listener if Jesus had said that a Pharisee came along and helped the poor man. But instead, in a shocking cultural reversal, Jesus described a Samaritan who stopped, helped, and cared for this Jewish man in such great need.

You have to understand the great divide between the Samaritans and the Jewish people to realize what a unique twist this is in the story that Jesus told. Samaritans were seen as "half-breeds," impure people with whom the Jews did not associate. During the exile, they had intermarried and developed their own modified Torah and temple worship and so were seen as "religious counterfeits" by the pure, chosen Jewish people. Jesus made His point with a person of prejudice and by challenging the cultural barriers of His audience.

That wasn't the only time He used this technique. In Matthew 5, Jesus also challenged the Jewish people to turn the other cheek after the Romans struck them, to walk two miles after being forced to walk one, and to give away their coats in addition to their shirts. Jesus was serious about demonstrating love to those who are not like us, and even toward those whom we dislike or those who hate us!

GETTING PERSONAL AT CHURCH

While I haven't found too many older people who would say that they hate the young people of the next generation, the divide is so great between them, and the distaste is sometimes so bitter, that they might as well admit it. They don't like the strange and confusing culture of those who are not like them: *their own young people!*

Many younger adults intimidate older adults because they don't know their language, their culture, or their interests (and they really don't want to learn). Sadly, love cannot be given or received in this situation.

On the other side of the equation, our society celebrates youth and despises age. That means today's youth rarely honor those who are older than them and tend to think they are the center of the world. Why? Because they're celebrated, marketed to, programmed for, and technologically enabled to see themselves as the center. Young people are not trained to appreciate their grandparents—many of them don't even know their grandparents, and even more never spend any time with anyone that old.

On top of all this, tragically, many families live together without love. They coexist in the same house without any tangible or visible expressions of love. They may use the words, but they still feel marginalized, ignored, and, in some cases, quite literally unloved. Communication is strained and understanding is rare.

Church families wrestle with these very same issues. Our church community is fractured if cross-generational love is not demonstrated. But this is what the church is called to do. We're called to be a place where all who follow Christ offer and receive love and understanding.

Transitional seasons are unavoidable in an organic, growing, and life-giving church. But massive cultural change that embraces a multigenerational mind-set requires intentional teaching and training, as well as relational connectivity from the pastor, to guide a church through this cultural change. Becoming truly multigenerational requires more than just tolerance of the other generations around us.

It requires something so much deeper. Sadly, many of our congregations are more concerned about their building, their worship style, or their traditions or lack thereof, and they get stuck in their own selfishness. This loveless disease can afflict the young as well as the old—it is no respecter of persons.

Young people may be just as addicted to soaring "U2-ish" electric guitar solos in worship as an older generation was to the great pipe organ. Any of us can get fixated on a certain style of worship as the most "authentic" or "anointed." That's why we need to respect heritage and history as well as be open to what the Holy Spirit is doing today. Worship is not defined by musical style but by the people worshipping together.

When we are not willing to shift our church culture over time, it's very much like a family in which the parents try to keep the kids from maturing. If the parents don't let them grow up and test their independence from time to time, their development will be stymied. Parents who never let their little kids try to walk for fear of hurting themselves actually create more danger for these little ones. Falling and failing are part of life, and teenagers need some room to grow so that they receive the experience of disappointment. If we don't provide enough input, stability, care, and concern during the turbulent teen years, children will end up with no foundation to ground them in life or in the family of God.

Sadly, many churches break apart under the burden of this kind of transition. It's too difficult for them to keep the family healthy—too chaotic and messy. Many faith communities find it much easier to create a corporate culture where a charismatic leader just hires and fires like a business. They find it more convenient to give people what they want, segment them, and manage them from a distance. But that approach doesn't acknowledge one irrepressible truth:

We all need to belong to a family.

EXPERTS AT LOVE

Of course, our churches are experts at so many wonderful things. We know how to program services and create experiences that draw people in. We understand worship teams and volunteer management. We've designed all kinds of children's services and youth-outreach programs. We're proficient at raising money and building new worship centers. We have experts in church growth and city reaching. We have specialists in reaching the next generation.

We tend to be a little too good at pinpointing the faults of others and judging sins, but, more importantly, there is one area of expertise that local church communities consistently struggle with, one chink in the armor of spiritual know-how and practical competence that holds us back. It is the central issue in our churches, but our seminars and conferences don't adequately teach us how to do it. I haven't heard many sermons on the topic, and there's a lack of resources for this particular task among the myriad of other training tools.

Jesus told a group of so-called spiritual experts that it was the most important of all the commands and in fact provided a framework for understanding and obeying all other commands (Matt. 22:34–40; Mark 12:28–34). This challenging issue for our churches and the missing ingredient in many of our worship services is love.

Our churches, indeed our people, need to be experts in the art of loving one another.

The seventh chapter of Luke paints one of the most beautiful pictures of love and devotion found in all of Scripture. If we look closely, we find the central theme of this story turns out to be two completely different kinds of people and their view of each other—opposite cultures coming together at, of all places, a dinner table.

In the story, Jesus accepted an invitation for dinner from Simon, the Pharisee. All seemed to be going well as dinner and conversation flowed at a leisurely pace—until the arrival of an uninvited guest. A woman "who lived a sinful life" (v. 37) somehow found her way into the house and stood behind Jesus. At first no one noticed her, but then she crumbled at Jesus's feet and began crying—just a little at first—but her cries grew into weeping and then sobbing.

Like this woman, so many in our current generation of young people are sad, depressed, or overwhelmed by disappointment. We have a whole generation of people who feel alone and isolated by divorce and family dysfunction. They are *love starved*. They don't have an advocate. Their parents are disinterested or unaware, and no one will invest in them. They are lost and lonely, just scrambling to make life work. However, when they find someone who is interested in them, such as a big brother or sister or a father figure from whom they sense sincere love, they open up wide, and a gush of passion, love, and gratitude begins to pour out. They soak it up like a dry and dusty sponge!

Look at what I mean as we go back to Luke 7.

Suddenly, the woman broke open a jar of perfume and began pouring it on Jesus's feet, wiping them with her hair. Then she started kissing them. Simon couldn't believe Jesus allowed this woman to touch him like that. And it almost appeared as if Jesus enjoyed it!

Just then, Jesus broke through the uneasiness and said, "Simon, I have something to tell you" (v. 40). Jesus told a story about two men whose moneylender canceled their debts—one man had a large debt and the other a small one. Jesus finished with a question: "Now which of them will love him more?" (v. 42). Simon, unnerved by the question, sensed that Jesus was up to something. Simon tried to sound convinced. "I suppose the one who had the bigger debt forgiven" (v. 43), he said.

Then Jesus described for Simon and everyone else in the room one of the secrets of honest, heartfelt, and life-giving love. It was right there for all of them to see, but they were embarrassed by the intimacy of it. It was uncomfortable. This woman had done something so beautiful for Jesus, and the only one who recognized its beauty and simplicity was Jesus Himself. Simon and the others got hung up on protocol and religious behavior. Jesus finished with this statement: "Her many sins have been forgiven—as her great love has shown. But whoever has been forgiven little loves little" (v. 47).

His statement hits me hard even now. Jesus described something that Simon wasn't close to understanding. You see, this story is not about the woman or how sinful she was. This story is about Simon's lack of love. Simon thought this woman's actions were inappropriate, but Jesus made the case for a depth of love that leads to extravagant devotion.

Many of our young people are extravagant worshippers. Sometimes they dress inappropriately, or they conduct themselves inappropriately, or they speak inappropriately in our churches. Some have never been trained, cared for, or encouraged. Frankly, teenagers and young people in general aren't always good at being humans yet—they haven't been at it as long as some of the rest of us. In fact, research says that their frontal lobes are not well developed until they get into their twenties. So they might do and say stupid things. They may act silly or break stuff. Sometimes they even ruin carpet or embarrass themselves in front of others.

"But this woman was doing what she was doing out of love, not silliness," you might argue. Yes, but the Pharisee didn't know that. Simon didn't have any tolerance for anything this woman did to love Jesus extravagantly. In a similar way, some of our churches just do not know how to provide for, encourage, or respect teenagers. The reason? We don't know how to love them.

First John 3:16 says, "This is how we know what love is: Jesus Christ laid down his life for us. And we ought to lay down our lives for our brothers and sisters." Love must be extravagant. Love is overwhelming, overtaking, and unrelenting. The very nature of love consumes. You can't love someone "a little." You can't "sort of" be in love with someone. Just ask your spouse. Either you are wildly, madly, and hopelessly in love, or you're not. I learned this lesson the hard way through an awkward courtship with my wife while we were both in college. I was scared of the commitment to marriage, and she was unwilling to give her heart to me completely unless I was willing to surrender to her love totally. Thank God I did! But I digress.

God defines love by giving His all through Jesus Christ and then letting us know that we should follow His example and surrender completely to love toward one another.

Further on in 1 John, chapter 4:11–12 says, "Dear friends, since God so loved us, we also ought to love one another. No one has ever seen God; but if we love one another, God lives in us and his love is made complete in us." The implication here is that we experience God through the love of other people. God is made real and present among us when we become experts in loving one another. This point is made clearer in 1 John 4:20–21: "Whoever claims to love God yet hates a brother or sister is a liar. For whoever does not love their brother and sister, whom they have seen, cannot love God, whom they have not seen. And he has given us this command: Anyone who loves God must also love their brother and sister."

The truth is that we cannot enter into worship and love God well if we've sentenced an entire demographic to love God separately from us because of our own selfishness. That goes the other direction as well. High-school and college students cannot despise their parents and grandparents and then try to love God extravagantly in their own "awesome" guitar-laden worship service. Love goes both ways.

But how do our young people learn this behavior of disrespect and desire for their own way? First of all, it is completely human to be selfish. Selfishness must be trained and disciplined out of us. But many young people learn bad behavior from dysfunctional parents or grandparents, especially if they're in a church that doesn't interact generationally. Of course, most of the time their attitude does not come from hatred or disgust; it's just selfishness, passivity, and ignorance. This segmentation and isolation belie a congregation consumed with its own desires instead of raising up the next generation.

How should the next generation learn to love others who are not like them? They are supposed to see it modeled in their parents, grandparents, mentors, and pastors. If they see love and life pouring out of us toward them, they will respond in kind when they grow up and begin having their own kids. Modeling is the chief way children are trained. Kids take our worst characteristics as parents and multiply them by a factor of ten. I've heard it said that what one generation tolerates, the next generation will exaggerate. Love is the great need in our church families. But it must start with those who are older. Culture is passed on through the actions, attitudes, and opportunities that the leaders of a church embrace. Our kids learn to love us because we've spent so much time loving them.

LOVE AND LONGEVITY

Worship is about loving God with all of our hearts, souls, minds, and strength (Mark 12:30), but it is impossible to enter into this kind of loving relationship with God unless we learn how to love one another. You wonder why worship is not powerful? Look around and see if people from different groups in your church love one another. Worship seems flat and uninspiring? It may not be the ability of the musicians; it may be the resounding gong or clanging cymbal you hear coming from the lack of love in your church (1 Cor. 13:1–3).

> If I speak in the tongues of men or of angels, but do not have love, I am only a resounding gong or a clanging cymbal. If I have the gift of prophecy and can fathom all mysteries and all knowledge, and if I have a faith that can move mountains, but do not have love, I am nothing. If I give all I possess to the poor and give over my body to hardship that I may boast, but do not have love, I gain nothing.

Back to the woman at Jesus's feet: She had probably been told by men all of her adult life that she was good for only one thing. And men like Simon inevitably told her that she was good for nothing. Her concept of love was no doubt warped and confused. But something happened to her. The compassion she saw in the eyes and actions of Jesus changed her heart. Her concept of love was transformed. The so-called inappropriate display of affection and devotion was actually a rebirth of knowing how to love purely, innocently, and totally. What was once strange and out of reach now became a surge of emotion and trust. This act was an outpouring of gratitude and joy that she had finally found love. And love had finally found her.

Every young person needs this in his or her life. Nothing can take the place of love—no amount of toys, events, or styles of music can change a person's heart like love.

Simon had no love in his heart for anyone but himself, and Jesus rebuked him for it. If we want our churches to be full of the presence of God, we must love one another like Christ loved us—totally, completely, and unreservedly. It's only when we become experts in loving the next generation that we will begin to see the strength and stability that build a legacy for our community of believers.

Simon was old enough, smart enough, and mature enough to have treated this woman differently. What we need in our communities of faith is for those who are older and more mature to lean toward the next generation instead of resisting or judging them.

It's crazy how some churches cater to the old and wise at the expense of the young and immature. Why would we force the most youthful and immature among us to embrace the needs of the most mature and wise among us? It doesn't make any sense! Those of us who have been matured and sobered by our life experiences and lessons need to pass them on. We must show them the way to self-lessness! We must model it for our kids because one day they will model it back to us—and to the next generation after them.

You see, love and longevity go hand in hand!

The next generation doesn't have to start over and learn the harsh lessons of life on their own. We cannot punish them by putting our wants and needs ahead of theirs. They can stand on the shoulders of our experience and wisdom. We can give them the greatest gift of success and succession. We can coach. We can mentor. We can help. We must help!

Love is the key. Love motivates us (2 Cor. 5:14), love covers over a boatload of sins (1 Pet. 4:8), love is patient and kind (1 Cor. 13:4), and love never fails (1 Cor. 13:8). Loving an older or a younger generation is the only way we can put up with their idiosyncrasies and behaviors. We've got to be motivated by something greater than our own styles, preferences, and needs. We must be motivated by the love of Christ and by our love for one another, which in turn makes us recognizable to the world as God's people.

TRUTH AND LOVE

In this chapter, I am describing the kind of love that the apostle Paul spoke of in Ephesians 4:15: "Instead, speaking the truth in love, we will grow to become in every respect the mature body of him who is the head, that is, Christ."

This verse implies that if we are willing to speak the truth in love, we can grow into maturity in Christ. I'm convinced that many

Christians, and churches for that matter, are stymied in their growth and maturity because they are unwilling to embrace truth and love.

Most churches embrace one or the other. There are communities that stand for truth, and despite the consequences, they're going to tell people exactly how it is. The truth is what sets people free, so they say, and consequently they emphasize truth to the detriment of love. This outlook of too much emphasis on truth, at the expense of love, tends to make the church mean and leads to legalism.

Other churches let love flow freely and never get around to the need to explain the truth. They think that love is all they need because God is love, and Jesus told us not to judge one another. Of course, that's a misrepresentation of Matthew 7, but they never seem to get around to speaking the truth that is needed for discipleship or correction. The result is a spiritually weak church that keeps people enslaved in their sin and ignorant of God's design for holiness and accountability in community. Love at the expense of truth is no love at all. Truth at the expense of love turns to tyranny.

At ONEchapel we have made Ephesians 4:15 a cornerstone scripture for our community because it applies to so many of our relationships. It reveals the core of discipleship and fuels evangelism. After all, no one cares how much truth we know if they think we're going to just beat them over the head with it. And people are convinced that we love them when we're willing to take a risk by gently, compassionately, and directly sharing the truth with them. I've heard it said that truth in love is meaningful, but love without truth is meaningless.

Creating a culture of love is required for truth telling; and truth telling is required for loving people well. Creating this kind of a church culture is hard work. It's a bit like having a best friend you don't want to hurt, but you know you've got to tell him the truth. You love him deeply, and that causes you to carefully and kindly confront him with the truth. Telling the truth is difficult, but most of us have more of a problem creating an atmosphere of love where trust is high and our confidence in others' motives is strong. We need to embrace both—a commitment to truth and an atmosphere of love. Both parents and grandparents are the role models for creating this culture in a family. If we tell the truth and create this culture of love, the next generation will do the same.

LOVE MAKES A HOUSE A HOME

When my family moved into the house we purchased this year, it seemed like a nice-enough house. It had ceramic tile throughout the downstairs level and a big family room upstairs. It was equipped with beautiful appliances and cabinetry. The fireplace was lovely and the rooms large and inviting, but somehow it still felt cold.

As we make memories in this house, it is warming up. The decorations on the walls; the first Christmas tree in the corner; the gatherings at our table (the same table, benches, and chairs that my wife, Aimee, ate at when she was a girl); even the broken pipes under the foundation that caused no running water for a week and the lawn that requires frustrating weeding—they all contribute to turning this house into a home.

But the primary element that contributes to making this house a home is love. Love fills the rooms and the hearts of our home. Love changes the atmosphere. Love redeems, rekindles, and recharges our family. Love connects the generations to our heritage. This love that we have for one another is tested every day, and it is challenged by our attitudes, words, and actions toward one another. We certainly aren't the perfect family, but our house is a home because we love one another.

I wonder if our churches could say the same thing. The stained glass, the pulpit and pews, the fellowship hall, the lobby or atrium, and the music—all of these things can feel cold, lifeless, and fruitless without the love of a gathering of believers. Love changes the atmosphere. Love defines our culture and creates opportunity for us to share real, honest, gut-wrenching truths. Love covers a multitude of sins, mistakes, and failures and is the pathway toward multigenerational ministry and mentoring. Love is the fuel that powers the great engine of our family heritage and history. Our houses of worship need to be filled with love and healing in order to make the house a home.

NOTES

1. Michael Emerson, cited in David Van Biema, "Can Megachurches Bridge the Racial Divide?" *Time,* January 11, 2010, www.time.com/time/magazine/article/0,9171,1950943-1,00.html.

Chapter 9

THE BROKEN FAMILY

LOVE AND LOSS

On Wednesday, November 1, 2006, a man accused my pastor, mentor, and friend of having a homosexual affair and taking drugs. At first I thought this was some political ploy. Ted was influential as the president of the National Association of Evangelicals, and the election season was upon us. I'll never forget the feelings of dread and fear washing over me as it became painfully obvious that some of the accusations were true.

As the senior associate pastor of a thriving fourteen-thousand-member church, I recall the unease of the staff as we gathered in the building we called "The Tent" on that fateful Thursday at New Life Church. I bore the responsibility of addressing the staff and letting them know that we were entering into a strange and unfamiliar process. I felt sick to my stomach—grief stricken and overwhelmed by the task before us.

During that day my memory jogged to a familiar feeling twenty years earlier when my own family had fallen apart, all of us struck by the pain of my parents' divorce. No matter what family you belong to, a violation of trust creates a wound that you never forget. God always has a way of healing us, but the memory lingers and is recalled by new pain.

The evening of that agonizingly long and grueling day, we held an emotionally draining elders' meeting. When it was over, I was more than ready to go home and try to fall asleep, attempting to escape the nightmare. Besides, I had a big day coming—the birth of our fifth child. It was 11:00 p.m. and there were still reporters hanging around. One reporter caught me on my way out the door and asked me for an interview. I obliged. There was no reason to keep it from them. The interview ran all day the next day. It was the first press interview admitting that some of the allegations were true.

I arrived home around midnight to my beautiful wife, Aimee, who was literally nine months pregnant. This was the child we didn't plan on. She never wanted to have five, but here we were, preparing to go to the hospital the next morning to welcome this little guy into the world—she would be induced at 7:00 a.m. The plan changed at 2:00 a.m. when Aimee woke me up and said, "It's time!" We got up and went to the hospital in the middle of the night.

We were beyond exhausted from the emotional upheaval, but as we all know, babies enter the world when they want to. Consequently, while CNN, FOX, MSNBC, ABC, CBS, PBS, and other networks carried the scandalous story, we sat cocooned in our little hospital room … alone, isolated, disappointed, and strangely numb, but waiting for our little miracle.

We certainly needed one.

LEADING THROUGH THE STORM

The next day, one of the overseers for our church, Pastor Larry Stockstill, called me at the hospital. By then, we were the proud parents of a beautiful baby boy, Owen Alexander (ten pounds, twenty-two inches long—my wife is amazing!). He asked me to come to the office where he and the other overseers were meeting.

I showed up in my jeans and a baseball cap, having stayed up all night through my wife's labor, still trying to recover from the sleep deprivation. I wondered what he would say.

It was another surreal moment in a long string of out-of-body experiences. I remember sitting there with four men as they weighed several decisions and discussed the church's future when Pastor Larry turned to me and said, "Can you lead this church through this?" It was such a big question that it seems silly now to think back on how quickly I answered. I already felt the supernatural grace that comes during these kinds of life-changing moments.

I looked him straight in the eye and said, "Yes, sir."

I had been on the phone from the hospital most of the last twenty-four hours while our church campus swarmed with broadcast trucks, and as satellite uplink dishes were set up all over our parking lot. It was a marathon weekend. Saturday night I arrived back at the hospital to spend a few quiet moments with Aimee and Owen. It was late, but I opened my laptop and began to type out the message that I would give to our church family the next morning. Even now, I can see the warm glow in the hospital room coming from the brass lamp in the corner while our sweet baby, Owen, slept in a little plastic rolling bin beside my rocking chair. After a whirlwind of activity, my body gave one last gasp of energy to put my thoughts down. I felt overwhelmed, but I have a distinct memory of the soothing comfort of the Holy Spirit as I prepared my remarks for the next morning.

I went home about midnight. My other four kids were in their beds while their godparents slept in my bedroom. The guest room would be my chamber of tortured sleep that night. As I trudged downstairs to the spare bedroom to sleep, I realized that I didn't have any underwear or socks for the next day. In approximately seven hours I would be speaking to more people than at any other time in my entire life because of the national broadcast—and I couldn't find my socks. That was pretty much a defining picture of my journey in that time.

I showed up early to church that day (with my socks on) and went to meet with the team that would share with the world our response to what had happened. I know the world wasn't necessarily watching that day. That sounds a bit self-absorbed, but *our* world as a family had collapsed, and we felt as if everyone wanted a piece of us. All of the major news organizations were there, and so we agreed on a press poolroom where everyone could pick up the live feed from one camera coming from our auditorium, which we called "The Living Room."

The family of New Life came to church in force that day, as did the curiosity seekers. People packed the room, along with the buzz of nervous energy. The sadness and questions hung in the air like a fog on a cold wintry day. It was my responsibility to open the service with prayer. That particular Sunday was scheduled for baby dedications. As crazy as it sounds, there were families down front prepared to have us pray over and dedicate their babies to the Lord. I'm not sure if they just didn't have cable television or what, but they were there with their babies dressed in beautiful laced outfits and new booties.

I walked to the podium and announced, "We're going to begin this Sunday just like we would any other. We're going to dedicate babies and worship together because that is what families do."

The place erupted in applause.

The fog lifted; we prayed over families and began to sing. We found ourselves worshipping with abandon. We wept and prayed that God would visit us in our hour of need. And He did, as He always does.

That day, I was installed as the interim senior pastor of New Life Church. I spoke of forgiveness. I shared in the sadness. I articulated the gospel message with all of the emotion and fortitude I could muster. I encouraged and challenged our church family to come together like never before.

They did. It was a beautiful display of New Life's foundations. It was truly a relational place with honest friendships and a commitment to the Scriptures. New Life did not have a celebrity-driven culture with a corporate atmosphere as so many churches do today. New Life Church was and is a genuine family. And in that time, we came together to comfort one another and to pull together like families do when a crisis comes. The sun broke through that dark day, but there were more clouds and rain ahead.

For the next ten months, this son of a preacher from a little town named Yakima, Washington, led the church with the most overwhelming and overcoming sense of grace. I was challenged like never before in my life, but God's hand sustained me. I was not especially prepared in any way for this moment in my life, yet I had been equipped as a very ordinary man to participate in something extraordinary.

All indications were that our church would be turned into a giant used-car parking lot.

But God had other plans.

New Life came together like the family that we had become. We continued with strength and courage and remained committed to reaching out to our community. It wasn't perfect and it wasn't very pretty, but God worked among us, and our church body not only survived but also thrived in the midst of the turmoil.

THE STORY OF OUR FAMILY

Today, New Life Church is a miracle! It is a thriving congregation and family that weathered several storms and discovered that their foundations are secure. Their faith is firmly built on the rock of Christ Jesus. This family of believers actually sponsored our church plant called ONEchapel, the church I pastor currently in Austin, Texas. We still have many friends and family members who have loved and supported us through the church-planting process, and we will always be grateful for their gracious encouragement and help. As I write these words, I'm heading back to speak to my New Life Church family.

I didn't think it would be honest to talk about church as family and then not reflect on one of the most public, if not influential, church-family breakdowns in our modern Christian era. I don't know that I am yet far enough away from it to identify all of the elements that led to the failure, and I am certainly not here to set any records straight, or hang out any dirty laundry. I don't want or need to explore the details of the scandal.

Conversely, I am deeply grateful for the ministry training, philosophy, and experience that I gained while ministering to the New Life Church family and serving under Pastor Ted Haggard for sixteen years. Many of these ideas shape ONEchapel even now in our fledgling beginning. I am part of this family, and I'm so grateful for the lessons, the love, and the life that we shared together. I wouldn't trade it for anything.

What I want to write about is how the family dealt with the crisis. I respect and appreciate what godly men tried to do in the official restoration process during the period after the accusations and dismissal of Pastor Ted. The overseers were a source of comfort and courage in their attempt to bring correction to a situation that none of them were prepared for. They all willingly surrendered countless hours, considerable effort, and financial cost to try to bring order to this chaotic crisis. I'll always be grateful for their tremendous effort and encouragement.

It was incredibly difficult to deal with the media scrutiny and the scandalous nature of the allegations. Since Ted was also the president of the National Association of Evangelicals, the controversy became the perfect storm of politics, religion, and homosexuality, creating an intensely challenging and charged environment—a trifecta of issues that made every move a news headline or a late-night talk-show joke. This was the backdrop for one of the most difficult jobs I've ever held, and the toughest family recovery of which I've ever been a part.

NO SUCH THING AS INTERIM

The Princess Bride is on my top-ten list of all-time favorite movies. The wit, charm, humor, and adventure make this a classic story for children of all ages. In one scene, Westley is explaining to Princess Buttercup the reason for his long absence and his adventures with the Dread Pirate Roberts, who had taken him prisoner on his ship as a slave. Each evening the Dread Pirate Roberts would say, "Good night, Westley. Good work. Sleep well. I'll most likely kill you in the morning."

And that is a pretty good description of what it feels like to be an "interim senior pastor." Especially in a situation where so much disappointment and suspicion existed, it became an atmosphere that was difficult to navigate. I had responsibility but not much authority. It is not a job I would recommend to anyone.

However, I did it because I loved that family. I had grown up in that family, and I wanted to help heal them and walk with them on the treacherous journey that was ahead. Families are worth saving, and I remained committed to doing all I could to save this one. As one of the older brothers, I took the position of protector, guide, encourager, and pastor. I didn't care what the title was; I *was* their pastor. And I deeply cared for these people and wanted to do everything I could to contribute to their healing.

The road ahead was demanding. The scrutiny of the media, the questions from the congregation, and the inquiries of the overseers combined for a heavy burden as we worked to rid ourselves of the long shadow created by Ted's deceit. We worked hard to restore trust to our family.

Trust is really all that a church has. Churches don't make widgets or products to buy and sell. Churches aren't supposed to be about selling God stuff or producing Christian products for the masses to consume. The church that Jesus is building is a family of relationships where the only currency is the good word of the leaders, as well as the people's trust. Integrity is the bedrock upon which the church is led, encouraged, and challenged by our leaders. This trust is the platform from which we serve.

BIBLICAL, RELATIONAL AUTHORITY

I've experienced the pain and disappointment of a violation of trust, but I was also on the receiving end of the stares, whispers, and accusations, which are equally as painful. Even though trust is the platform from which we lead, leaders still make mistakes. It's impossible for leaders to live a perfect life, and we cannot hold them to an impossible standard. Imperfection goes along with any organization that's full of people. However, when we put our leaders on a pedestal, they have nowhere to go but down. It's not fair to our leaders, and it's an illusion for the people who put them there. Because we are imperfect leaders, we must be willing to surrender to relationships and authority in order to protect integrity and guard people's trust. We need to allow others the opportunity to speak into our lives about sensitive and difficult subjects so that confidence fills the hearts of those who follow us.

I don't believe in trying to create accountability. I believe in relationships where accountability is the by-product. If we try to set up accountability without relationship, we'll be tempted to hide our failures. If we build relationships with those whom we love, we won't want to lie. We'll endure painful truth because love is at stake. Accountability without relationship can easily turn into empty legalism and broken rules. But relationships filled with love create the seedbed for honesty and integrity.

Most great pastors I know lead with a limp. They have experienced a brokenness in their lives that has taught them humility. This humility opens the door to relationships and vulnerability, and helps them to treat other people with respect, love, and mercy.

Authority must be held with this same humility. However, the very nature of someone who holds the ability to correct, rebuke, and instruct can put the fear of the Lord in us. This is as it should be, because authority is about protection. As one wise person said,

"Submission doesn't begin until there is disagreement." This is where church-government structures often go awry. Church authority typically comes in one of two categories: either it is overbearing and harsh, or it is distant and disengaged. Neither is biblical. The authority figures encouraged in the Bible are ones who nurture and create an atmosphere of love from which to speak truth (Eph. 4:15). They are the ones who gently restore a brother who has fallen (Gal. 6:1). And they are to take responsibility as ones who must give an account (Heb. 13:17).

I'm not sure anyone should go to a church where there are not obvious, relational, and accountable authority figures to whom the pastor can submit. It is true that anyone can lie, and no accountability is foolproof no matter how invasive or extensive. But that's why there must be real, relational, and biblical authority in place. Biblical authority is based on relationships that really matter. Hearts knit together. Friends. Love. Surrender. These are the terms of biblical, relational authority.

I truly believe that if I demonstrate my willingness to surrender to biblical and relational authority in my life, that my church—the people who come to ONEchapel—will be more likely and more willing to yield their lives to my leadership. Why? Because they feel safe. The practice of healthy, biblical, and relational authority helps to protect us as leaders. God's idea of authority and oversight in the Scriptures is not about control, governance, or power. It's simply about protection. Protection for ourselves, from ourselves, and protection for the people we lead.

Biblical, relational authority should come from a position of deep love and grace. It is a relationship that is defined by the desire to protect and defend. In a word, it is *fatherly*. It is familial, not corporate. It doesn't concern itself with the assets first and the person second. Biblical, relational authority must be earned and argued for as the apostle Paul did in 2 Corinthians. Permission must be given and openness offered. It cannot be taken or demanded. Biblical, relational authority is what Moses cultivated with the people of Israel. His authority was fragile at times, and there were fights and frustrations along the way, but it was a relationship based on love and trust. Romans 13 says all authority has been given by God and is useful for protecting those who do right. It is also used to punish those who do wrong. If we do right, we can feel safe. If we do wrong, we should be afraid. That's the way it's supposed to be!

This is where the relationship usually breaks down. But I maintain that if there is a relationship already intact, this fear, while justified, is also accompanied by love, encouragement, and grace. The offender may well be disciplined, but because of the relationship, the offender extends trust to the authority figure. It is true that some authority figures are not relational and tend to respond to failure in an unbiblical way, but that should not undo our commitment to healthy, mature, biblical, relationally driven, and God-given authority. We can't undo the principle because of the exceptions or abuses.

I don't think anyone enjoys structures that hamstring our ministries with needless bureaucracy so as to keep our leaders accountable. However, as leaders, we do well when we demonstrate our submission to Christ by willingly surrendering our lives to another person for relational authority and guidance. No one can make us do anything. We choose to obey God or not, and when we don't, we need loving, caring authority figures to challenge us and lead us into repentance.

When we choose not to repent, we will suffer the consequences of broken relationships, dysfunctional churches, and wounded families.

DYSFUNCTIONAL CHURCH FAMILIES

The situation at New Life Church lacked true relational authority and guidance. Not because the overseers were not willing to provide it, but because they *could not* provide it. In my view, the relationships with the outside overseers were strained at times and surface level at best. We ended up with a dysfunctional family because of the deception and hiddenness of a stronghold in Ted's life. I knew Ted was not a perfect man, but I never knew the level of the deception. Many of our young staff members worked in an environment where the leadership exemplified many wonderful and influential ministry truths. Our church culture was highly relational and loving. There was honesty and trust among the staff, but there was also a growing deception. As the truths grew in our lives like wheat for the harvest, so the tares grew up right beside them. I believe that this is why there was such great pain and disappointment among our staff. The shock and dismay were the result of suddenly realizing that our relationships weren't as honest and committed as we thought.

Many churches across the landscape of our twenty-first-century American culture are truly dysfunctional. Some are harsh, legalistic, and authoritarian in their response to people's sin. Some are permissive, greasy grace giving, and powerless. The answer to this dysfunction is somewhere in the middle, which, as all of us know, is a challenging place to find.

My journey led me to the realization that the pastor and father of our church, Ted, had become increasingly dysfunctional over time, as addicts always do. In the last year of Ted's tenure at the church, his behavior became more erratic and confusing. Ted himself has said that he tried to overcome his own sinful desires and achieved victory over them for significant periods of time. But he could not sustain his strength under the crushing weight of the size and influence of his ministries. The pressure became too great and began to trap him. It seems obvious now, but no one could see it clearly then. There was no one in Ted's life who was both relational and authoritative. There was authority, but it was not truly relational. There were relationships, but none in authority over him.

In a natural family, if one of the members becomes dysfunctional, sometimes it may become necessary for the family members to separate for a period of time. This is especially true of situations where the dad, mom, or even a child becomes abusive, self-destructive, or harmful to self or to others. This ensures that the family stays safe during the healing process and gives the offender time to heal and demonstrate repentance. Every addict will try to lie his or her way out of the situation. Deception becomes a way of life, and the family accumulates coping skills that are typically unhealthy. This required separation is an extremely challenging and tenuous process as every relationship is tested. The offender, the offended, and each family member will have a perception that can lead to disagreement, frustration, fear, and more mistrust.

I've seen this dysfunction happen in marriages and families throughout my ministry life, and I think it's part of what happened at New Life Church at the beginning of the process. As events unfolded, Ted's lack of relationship with people in authority began to show, and the bridge to real restoration could not be crossed.

CULTURAL DISTINCTIVENESS

Each of our families has cultural norms. We develop them through time, personality, and experiences. For example, my family of origin wasn't very good at discussing difficult issues. My dad was a very strong personality but struggled with receiving input and communication. My mom was very loving but struggled with her own self-esteem. After my parents' divorce, my dad remarried and our new family culture completely flipped. The new blended family was overcommunicative, loud, and obnoxious. That's what happens when you have five teenagers living in the house. When my wife, whose family is reserved and proper, met my family, she thought we were crazy. Of course, we were and are, but that's not the point here.

Each family has its own culture, and this culture spills over into the extended family culture. They all enjoy some of the same food, traditions, vacations, and hobbies because they're all ultimately connected to Grandma and Grandpa. However, extended families such as aunts, uncles, and cousins often develop their own unique cultural distinctiveness over time because of the way they raise children, where they settle geographically, what kind of job they do, and how much money they make. The large extended families have overlapping cultural norms because they have the same origin. Grandparents and parents teach their children the same cultural values, but those values morph inside of each family unit.

In our case, my family of origin was quite different from all of our uncles, aunts, and cousins because we believed in different spiritual values, lived in an urban setting versus a rural setting, and in addition, they were all much older. We were unique in our own family units, but all of us shared the family name and some of the same traits. I've seen my dad stand just like my grandpa with his hand just above his hip, leaning on it with his elbow sticking out. Strangely enough, I've also caught myself standing in this exact same pose from time to time, and I always stop it quickly. To me it looks like an old man. It looks like my grandpa!

You might be able to identify with vowing never to raise your kids the way your parents, brother, or sister raised their kids. We all have had a moment when we've said (or it has been said about us), "Wow, they should really get a hold of those kids and discipline them. Let's make sure we never raise our kids like that!" This is the cultural and relational difference that shows up in a large extended family. But the more overlap there is culturally, the more relational connectivity there is, and vice versa. When crisis hits, it stretches that fabric of the family relationships and in some cases tears it. Families pull apart more easily when the relational fabric is weak and the cultural values are unclear. But when there is a strong relational fabric, a crisis cannot do so much damage and affirms the bonds of the family.

LACK OF A SHARED CULTURE

There are many reasons why the official and original restoration process failed and the relationships severed. I don't pretend to know them all, but one of the reasons that this family fractured during the period after the scandal is because of the unfamiliar cultures and lack of relationship. Of course, there was a perceived relationship with each of those in authority over Ted, but there was no real relational authority that could stand the test of this offense. Ted's influence had risen to a level that was both intimidating and separating. Books, TV appearances, and weekly calls from the White House created that separation. This caused a lack of genuine connection, relationship, and ultimately submission. We saw those overseeing pastors only when we were dedicating a building or hosting a pastors' conference that they attended. The only way the overseers could have done anything differently is if Ted had invited them into a more personal and cultural connection early on in the life of the church.

That is why the overseers called in three other very high-profile pastors with large ministries to challenge, encourage, and corral Ted. It proved even more difficult than originally thought. The family disconnect was relational, cultural, and spiritual, and it became too overwhelming.

Every church needs an authentic extended family with overlapping culture, authority, and relationships. At New Life, there was no extended family. There weren't enough overlapping family experiences or cultural norms. The fabric of the relationships was too strained. If there would have been a greater relational quotient in the authority and a greater cultural connection between Ted and the men he chose as his overseers, the restoration process—which is difficult regardless of the relationship—might have stood a better chance at succeeding. The lack of a cohesive culture and a genuine relational authority helped doom the restoration.

GENERATIONAL OVERLAP

Why is this important? Because in order to have a family church with multiple generations represented, there must be a cohesive culture to which everyone subscribes. We need grandparents, parents, aunts, uncles, and cousins involved so that we can be trained well, protected carefully, and cared for in crisis.

At the same time, we need to learn from others who are not in our family. I practice a leadership style that says we can't learn everything from someone, but we can learn something from everyone. The goal is to develop a family culture within our churches from top to bottom that encourages dialogue, attentiveness, humility, connectedness, and respect. As pastors, we birth a family culture by including in our church family those people we want to speak into our lives. We invite people we respect and love to speak into our family of believers. They become like grandparents, or aunts and uncles, to our local family. They can be consulted for wisdom, and encouraged to give us feedback and protection in a crisis. If each of our congregation members knows these people in authority and how they function within the context of our own church family, they feel safe.

During the first year of our church plant I invited each of our overseers to speak to our congregation because I want their influence in our family. The overseers are not governmental to our church—the internal elders perform that role—but they are relational overseers and have authority in my life. That means that I want their influence, and naturally, I want some of their overlapping culture to spill into our church culture. I believe in relational authority that influences how I lead, and gives guidance that creates strength, protection, and accountability.

Are there risks involved? Yes. Are there weaknesses in all of our families? Yes. I understand there are risks and weaknesses with every church-government structure. But I'd rather take the risks associated with relationships and family than a misplaced confidence in an ironclad governmental structure. The benefit of doing church as family is greater than that of doing ministry alone and building a self-absorbed kingdom. The risks of dysfunctional and messy families are worth the price of protection, submission, and love. That is the strength of a genuine family. Grandparents, parents, brothers, sisters, aunts, uncles, and cousins all create a fabric of encouragement, love, and safety. We need the power of generational influence, both up and down through the family. New Life Church had some of these relationships internally but no relationships of authority externally, and when a very rainy day occurred, *we got swept away.*

New Life Church remains healthy and strong despite the storm and, today, is a light to that community, but it took a toll on the family, as sin always does. Brady Boyd, the new senior pastor, did an incredible job leading through the very difficult days that were to come for New Life Church. But at the end of the day, he was not originally related to this family. He married in as a stepdad, and that relationship always takes a considerable amount of time to build.

I know. I'm from a blended family myself.

Chapter 10

THE BLENDED FAMILY

THE FAMILY CHALLENGE

I saw the name come up on the screen of my Treo smartphone, and my heart skipped a beat. At that moment, I was driving toward the church, nine months into a grueling leadership position as the interim senior pastor with a lot of responsibility but not much authority. I was tired of wondering what was going to happen, tired of fielding awkward questions from staff and congregation members.

It was Lance Coles, our church administrator, my longtime friend, and head of the Pastoral Search Committee. He asked me to come to a meeting to get the answer to this long-overdue question of who would be chosen to lead New Life Church into the next season. I didn't want to go to a meeting. I wanted to know.

So I pressed him to tell me.

Lance Coles is one of the unsung heroes of the New Life family. He probably endured more pain, struggle, and criticism than any of the rest of us. He is the kind of man who does the right thing no matter what. He is attentive to every detail, and thoughtful and committed to the outcome that will serve people best. He never quits. He never gives up, and he is incredibly loyal. He endured, got little recognition, and is one of the heroes who carried New Life through its most challenging time.

On the phone that day, he didn't want to tell me. He didn't want to do it this way, but after my appeal to his best intentions to help me as I was preparing to depart for a much-needed family vacation, he relented.

"Ross, I'm so sorry, but you didn't get it," he said.

I was stunned.

Truly, the signs had been obvious over the past few months. If I were going to be the new pastor, there would have been an altogether different energy and momentum as that summer progressed. Down in the depths of my spirit, I knew. I had preached every Sunday for the last two months knowing that I probably wouldn't get the job, but it didn't make the moment any easier.

I had chosen to be a candidate only because I thought it might best serve the church's continuity and culture. I had received many other opportunities in the past to go and lead another congregation, but had never received what I thought was the green light from the Holy Spirit to leave New Life. I wondered if this opportunity might be the reason why. But honestly, I didn't know for sure. God would not let me look into the future. The road forward was cloudy, but still I forged ahead, trying to do my best to be a good steward of every moment.

Finally, this moment had come and it was painful. I knew the public embarrassment that I would feel if I were not chosen, but I also knew that if I couldn't stand the heat of that prospect, I should just get out of the proverbial kitchen. Lance tried to explain the agony of the decision. It didn't matter. We talked for a few more moments, and then we hung up. I sat in stunned silence for a few minutes. I dialed Aimee and told her. We really didn't know how to respond in the moment. I could hear her quiet disappointment as I sat on the side of the road on the north side of Colorado Springs, letting out some of the pent-up emotion inside. A sense of relief would come, but that moment was challenging. I really didn't know what to do next. Suddenly, I remembered why I was on my way to the church. As the host pastor, I was supposed to give the opening prayer and welcome at the Desperation Conference to six thousand students and leaders.

I was desperate indeed. I showed up at the conference, provided the opening invocation, stood at the back for a few minutes watching the miracle of thousands of teenagers worshipping with abandon in our church. Yes, our church that had been through this wilderness of scandal and pain. The thought of God's grace on us made the moment even more painful for me, if that makes any sense. I went home soon after that. We were getting ready for a two-week family vacation to south-central Texas to see Aimee's mom and family. Just in time!

You have to grasp the depth of the family relationship at New Life Church to understand the pain of this situation. We were the church that was real, earthy, and relational. We really were a family and that's why I felt crushed. It's also probably why I could endure this public rejection. I loved our family of believers. I loved Ted and each and every staff member, all of whom became more like brothers and sisters than colleagues. We ate together, vacationed together, and worked together. We believed in this family. I still do. I am still convinced that our model of relational ministry was not a failure. It was a success, and that's why New Life still stands to this day.

I proceeded to work through the process of what to do next. Would I stay at New Life with a new pastor? I realized very quickly that there was no way I could just leave the church as a result of not being chosen. I couldn't leave the family while they were getting to know a new pastor—*a new dad*.

I remember my good friend Rob Brendle, one of the New Life pastors and now senior pastor of Denver United, saying to me these harsh and yet strangely encouraging words. He said, "It looks like you're going to have to go all the way to the cross on this one." What he meant was that I was not going to be able to save myself any dignity. I had put myself out there as a candidate, and I was going to have to endure the full treatment of public humiliation, as Christ did. In some ways, there was going to be a death for me. But thankfully, and as always when God is working, there would also be a resurrection.

MEETING MY FUTURE

I've always enjoyed eating at Chili's. There are few things in this world quite as wonderful as their chips and queso, and Chicken Crispers. Not the healthiest thing on their menu (or any menu), but oh, so good! Chili's was the site of a life-changing moment for me, but it didn't have anything to do with food.

My wife grew up in New Braunfels, Texas. Thirty years ago, her dad planted a church there called Tree of Life Fellowship, and today, her brother, Don Duncan Jr., pastors that church. For sixteen years we made the annual trek from Colorado Springs to south-central Texas. We would enjoy The Schlitterbahn, the world's number-one water park, according to the Travel Channel. We made the rounds to the Alamo, the capital in Austin, Fiesta Texas, and tubing the river. It's a great vacation destination!

We tried to unwind after the search committee had made the decision. In a way, I felt relief at no longer carrying the weight of not knowing. But after such a long, arduous journey we found ourselves more weary and unsure of the future than ever. I really didn't know how to respond to this newfound sense of freedom. However, it wasn't just the end of one season of the unknown; it was the beginning of a brand-new season of unknowns.

Brady Boyd was the senior associate pastor at Gateway Church in Southlake, Texas, where Robert Morris is the senior pastor. Brady had helped develop, train, and pastor the leadership team of Gateway from its beginnings as a church of about two hundred people. The church exploded in seven years of grace-filled ministry to over ten thousand people. Brady came from good stock and training.

My first conversation with Brady came after he left me a message on my cell phone. He was excited at the prospect of moving from the Texas heat to the clean, crisp air of Colorado Springs.

I was not excited to speak to him.

Honestly, I felt drained, deflated, and defeated. The last thing I wanted to do was talk to the guy who was taking the job that I was already doing.

He persisted.

Finally, I called him back and we met each other on the phone—*awkward*. I was scheduled to speak at the National Worship Leader Conference in Austin, Texas, that week, and he asked if he could come down and meet with me. The team at New Life was anxious to see if we could find common ground so that we might work together. I begrudgingly obliged. It's not that I was mad, just disappointed. I struggled to find the reason and the meaning.

Brady Boyd and Tom Lane, Gateway's associate senior pastor, flew down from Dallas to Austin and showed up at the Worship Conference to meet with Glenn Packiam and me. I drove my father-in-law's white 1997 two-door Continental Mark VII to the conference, since it was just an hour away from New Braunfels. This low-riding, long white automobile was not the kind of car you want to make a good impression with. I sent Glenn Packiam, who was with me, to get the car washed while I taught two sessions at the conference. We would meet up with them at the church and go together to lunch at Chili's.

The whole thing was very strange. Brady was my age and a peer, and Tom Lane was older and more fatherly. I'll never forget Brady and Tom, who are both bigger-framed men, folding into the backseat of that low-riding Continental. Awkward pauses and small talk continued until we got to the restaurant. We squeezed into a booth and started really talking. I shared my struggle and disappointment about the journey. But I assured them that I was committed to the people of New Life Church. From the get-go Brady made it clear that he wanted me to stay at New Life and walk through this transition together.

I knew that it was probably in his best interest to say this, but I vividly remember a puzzling sense of calm that washed over me as we sat and listened. We genuinely shared fellowship as we broke bread together. Jesus was with us as we ate at Chili's, and we left wondering how this might work, but oddly encouraged at the same time.

When this kind of situation develops at a church, it is customary for the team in place to stay so that the transition can happen smoothly until the senior pastor has a chance to get situated. Eventually, the staff is expected to bow out gracefully at the appropriate time to allow the new leader to build his own team.

I didn't know what to expect when we got home to Colorado Springs. How would I integrate with Brady? How would I feel facing the congregation after it became known that I wasn't chosen? What would it be like to work with a peer? How would we navigate the road ahead? These questions and a million more flooded my mind—it didn't turn out to be much of a vacation after all.

Our family came home from that trip and hit the ground with many meetings and discussions about how the process would unfold. Larry Stockstill, the head overseer, asked me to speak to the congregation on my first Sunday back.

It was in that moment of speaking to the family of New Life Church that I shared my faith in God's direction for my life. I was still pastoring them, and this was as powerful of an illustration as I could present to them as they watched this drama of my life unfold before their eyes. They were, after all, interested in who would be their next pastor.

Proverbs 16:9 says, "In their hearts humans plan their course, but the LORD establishes their steps." I couldn't imagine what would be next for me, but I was sure that God knew. A calmness came over me that I could not explain. After all that we'd been through, I trusted God.

Most leaders who come into an organization after a scandal of that magnitude would have built a new team quickly. Most pastors who take the reins of a church don't want to keep their competition for the job around!

Brady didn't do that with me. He was gracious and listened carefully to my story. He allowed me to process and grieve. He gave me space and time to heal up. He encouraged me and gave me opportunities to lead and share. Brady reached out to me and we forged a genuine friendship. It was tenuous at first, but we both knew that this family needed pastoring, and we were committed to them.

It turns out that Brady and I became real friends. We became grateful for each other, and that began to set the tone for the rest of the family: the staff, the elders, the leaders, and the congregation. It was a path I had never walked before, and we learned a lot about who we were as a family and who God was shaping us to become.

GOD'S BLENDED FAMILY

One of the decisions that the search committee of New Life Church had to make as they began to look for the next leader of the church family was were they going to choose the elder brother within the family to lead the church, *namely, me*? Or were they going to choose someone outside the family and essentially find a new dad to marry into the family, so to speak?

I know that they prayed, fasted, and spent countless hours doing their best to find the mind of the Lord on this decision. They interviewed several candidates, consulted with many experts and pastors, and then decided on the best course of action following the Lord.

I believe they succeeded.

It was painful, but they made the right call. I don't know what choosing me would have created, though I like to think it would have been successful. At the end of the day, I believe God rescued me from a potentially impossible situation. He gave me a different path—as only He can.

At first glance, you might think that I'm using this analogy of a stepfather and marriage in a negative way, but I am not. I know the challenges of blended families, but I also know their strengths. Many stepfathers and stepmothers are a godsend to their stepchildren and stepfamilies. Stepparents who adopt are oftentimes the only mom or dad a child knows. They bring stability, peace, and strength into a difficult family situation.

This is the case with Brady.

My own father became a true blessing to the children of my stepmom when they married. And my stepmom genuinely became a source of love and acceptance to my two brothers and me. We didn't all get along right away, and there were many moments of testing authority and misunderstood communication. But somehow in the midst of two broken families, one emerged that was healthier, stronger, more open, and generally warmer than the original family. Out of the ashes of two grieving families came the miracle of one beautifully blended family.

This is also the story of New Life, and if you look carefully, it is the story of the Bible. New Life needed a steady and consistent hand at the plow in the aftermath of the loss of a beloved pastor. Our church needed an extended family that would provide love, wisdom, experience, and resources. We found that in Gateway Church in Southlake, Texas. We've become extended family with that community of believers, and Pastor Robert Morris came to New Life several times early on to cross-pollinate vision and values. We found another extended family member in one of Brady's father figures, Jimmy Evans from Trinity Fellowship Church in Amarillo, Texas. Pastor Jimmy visits New Life consistently and continues to give great guidance and insight to that family of believers, both behind the scenes as well as in their services. New Life has certainly benefited from the strength of these other families, and I believe those churches have experienced the grace of New Life Church, with all the energy, enthusiasm, and innovative ideas that the New Life family embodies.

JEWS AND GENTILES

If you think about the promise in Genesis 12 given to Abraham and his descendants, God's first chosen family, there was always a plan to include other families. The Abrahamic covenant was a promise to bless the family so that they could bless other families. Ultimately, this blessing came through Joseph, Moses, David, and Jesus. The apostle Paul made it clear in Romans 9–11 that it was always God's plan to merge the two households of the Jews and Gentiles and make them into one blended family. Look at what he wrote in Ephesians 2:11–19:

> Therefore, remember that formerly you who are Gentiles by birth and called "uncircumcised" by those who call themselves "the circumcision" (which is done in the body by human hands)—remember that at that time you were separate from Christ, excluded from citizenship in Israel and foreigners to the covenants of the promise, without hope and without God in the world. But now in Christ Jesus

you who once were far away have been brought
near by the blood of Christ.

For he himself is our peace, who has made
the two groups one and has destroyed the barrier,
the dividing wall of hostility, by setting aside in
his flesh the law with its commands and regula-
tions. His purpose was to create in himself one
new humanity out of the two, thus making peace,
and in one body to reconcile both of them to God
through the cross, by which he put to death their
hostility. He came and preached peace to you who
were far away and peace to those who were near.
For through him we both have access to the Father
by one Spirit.

Consequently, you are no longer foreigners and
strangers, but fellow citizens with God's people and
also members of his household.

Did you see it? This is the heart of God. Jesus created in Himself
one new humanity out of the two! He broke down the dividing walls
and barriers, making families out of strangers. He welcomes the alien
and the stranger into His family. Notice the beautiful invitation God
extends through the prophet Isaiah in 56:3–8:

"Let no foreigner who is bound to the LORD say,
"The LORD will surely exclude me from his people."
And let no eunuch complain,
"I am only a dry tree."

For this is what the LORD says:

"To the eunuchs who keep my Sabbaths,
who choose what pleases me
and hold fast to my covenant—
to them I will give within my temple and its walls
a memorial and a name better than sons and daughters;
I will give them an everlasting name
that will endure forever.
And foreigners who bind themselves to the LORD
to minister to him,
to love the name of the LORD,
and to be his servants,
all who keep the Sabbath without desecrating it
and who hold fast to my covenant—
these I will bring to my holy mountain
and give them joy in my house of prayer.
Their burnt offerings and sacrifices
will be accepted on my altar;
for my house will be called
a house of prayer for all nations."
The Sovereign LORD declares—
he who gathers the exiles of Israel:
"I will gather still others to them
besides those already gathered."

God invited foreigners into the family. The childless received
sons and daughters. Those who loved the Lord and bound themselves

to His covenant, no matter where they came from, He blended into this family. He invited the nations of the world into the house of prayer. This is God's heart and His desire all through the Scriptures, and even today. He wants a people He can call His own, and He used the analogies of marriage, unfaithfulness, love, and even divorce throughout the Old Testament. The blended family shows God's gracious love and mercy in the midst of an imperfect and broken world. He loves to place broken people without a family into the loving and protecting family that is the church.

Stop and meditate on Psalm 68:5–6:

> A father to the fatherless, a defender of widows,
>   is God in his holy dwelling.
> God sets the lonely in families.

There is no more beautiful picture of God's desire for family than this. He will be a father, He will defend the widow, and He will set the lonely in families. This is our calling in a world where people suffer from the pain of divorce and feel isolated from their natural families. So many feel alone and without hope. Their families are broken, and they have been wounded by the sins and violations of their fathers and mothers. God calls us to encourage people that they belong, and that they are welcome in His family. That's what our churches must be. God's family includes all kinds of people, and we need more and more churches that will welcome the lonely into their families.

That's why I am planting a new church in Austin, Texas.

But I'm not doing it alone. I have help. I belong to a family.

PLANTING A NEW FAMILY

One of the strengths brought to our family table by Pastor Brady was what I have begun to identify as the ability to "Celebrate the Sending." New Life had never been much of a "sending" church, although we have sent our share of pastors and missionaries, both short and long term, into the fields of harvest. We certainly believed in a mission mind-set, and we shared in praying, training, and encouraging people to go. But the actual departure was always painful. It felt more like a parting of the ways than a sending. It resembled more of a family divorce than a marriage celebration.

Brady began to articulate the idea of how we should celebrate God's calling to be sent out as a family. This is how it happens in a family when there is a marriage. Children grow up, they mature, and they meet another person with whom they want to start their own family. Families plan a ceremony, make a guest list, send invitations, and the marriage becomes a celebration of love between two hearts joining two families. Yes, Mom cries through the ceremony, and Dad sheds a tear as he kisses the bride and gives her away. But sadness is only a small part of the event, and the joy of a new life together overshadows everything else.

A marriage therefore represents both sorrow and happiness for the family. This is how a church should feel when they send one of their own to plant. This is how Aimee and I felt when we were sent out from New Life Church as church planters in the spring of 2010. There was part of me that didn't want to leave, but I knew that God wanted me to go on to the next season of my life. I was excited to strike out on my own, but also knew that I needed the blessing and prayers of my family.

Truth be told, I was scared to death to give up a successful career and a position of influence. God had blessed me over eighteen years of grace-filled worship ministry. I made a commitment when Pastor Brady took the job as senior pastor that I would hold steady and consider spending the rest of my life as part of this beautiful New Life family. For a while, I thought that might be my path. I had credibility as a pastor who had weathered the storm. I had the love of friends and years of investment in the community. I had the opportunity to make music and train worship leaders. I had started a worship school and stewarded the songwriting and recordings of New Life Worship.

But as my heart began to heal from the pain and disappointment, I couldn't shake the feeling of wanting to lead a community and shape a new family of believers. I wanted to be spiritually challenged again and find my own way to the next season of my life and ministry. I didn't want to leave, but I did want to start something new!

As I tentatively began to share this with Pastor Brady, I wasn't sure how he would respond. Would he throw me out and bless me publicly, but curse me privately as so many pastors do? Would he resist? Would he help me figure it out? I really wasn't sure of anything at that point. I was in a strange and unfamiliar territory as I came up to that moment of talking to Pastor Brady about what was going on inside my heart.

And then I realized Brady began to do for me what others had done for him. He didn't want me to leave, but he began to pray with me about my process as I invited him into it. We touched base about once a month on the subject of planting a church. We prayed about a new role for me, or possibly taking over an existing church. I had watched Brady do that, and I had already sung that song. I really didn't think there was any chance of my trying to captain another ship that was already sailing. We talked about starting a national ministry of worship training and resourcing, but nothing felt right to me, except for starting another family.

A few months into the process, we asked the elders to pray about my sense of the next chapter coming in my life. I had identified Austin as a possible destination because it was close to family, needed more life-giving churches, and featured a warm climate. I wasn't sure, but once we traveled for a second time to pray through the city, I began to believe that this was God's calling for us. The elders agreed and we continued to pray together. Three months later we put our house on the market, and eleven months after my initial discussion with Brady, we told the church our decision. Our house sold in three months, in a terrible real-estate market and for the full asking price. We left Colorado Springs in February 2010.

Brady is not a father figure in my life, but he played the role of a father as he surrendered to the process of this sending-out, this marriage celebration. He's kind of like my older brother, looking out for me and taking care of my family. He and the elders of New Life Church sent me out with prayers of blessing, a bunch of families that moved with us, and a generous amount of cash. It was a celebration with a twinge of sadness, just as it should be with a loving family.

YOUR CHURCH CAN BE A FAMILY

No matter what kind of church you come from, God can make you into a family. No matter where you've been in the past, God can place you in His family.

Some churches have been ripped apart by fear or failure, but God can heal and restore your spiritual family. You may be part of a church that's recovering from a scandal, a violation, a split, or a falling-out. God wants to put you back into a family. He wants to put your church family back together.

It can happen.

I've seen it.

You might be the one who feels lonely and isolated in your spirituality. God has a home for you. You might be afraid to take the risk again, but I'm telling you that it is worth it! You might have become cynical and wounded from a bad family situation in your church. God wants to melt your heart and join you to a community of grace that will walk with you on your faith journey. No matter what has happened to you or how you've been hurt, I'm here to tell you that the faithfulness and love of God are available to heal your heart. He healed mine.

No community is perfect. The house isn't always clean. The dinner table is loud and messy sometimes, and it is certainly not convenient to belong to a family. But you were not meant to do this alone. You were made for community. God designed you to love and be loved.

God loves you.

And you belong to His family.

A MULTIGENERATIONAL CHURCH SERVICE MODEL (THE FIVE Cs)

I would like to introduce you to an idea that came to me as I was teaching at the New Life School of Worship in Colorado Springs several years ago. I was taking the students through the many centuries of worship styles and experiences since the early church and had to translate for them why we "do" worship the way it's done in the twenty-first-century American church. Most traditional churches have tried to put together contemporary worship services or add modern elements to their liturgy, but not many modern worship ministries have tried to add historical and liturgical elements to their current charismatic experiences. Having been influenced by Robert Webber's ancient-future concept and Glenn Packiam's experiments in his New Life Services, ONEchapel has tried to connect the old and the new to become "rooted in history while leaving room for the mystery of the Holy Spirit among us." Here are five ideas for integrating old and new, helping our church reach back while moving forward.

CREEDS
Creeds have been used in church life for centuries as a way of training people and reminding them of what they believe. Later, songs with theological statements and principles accomplished the same

task of teaching people who God is and what the Bible says. The songs our churches use can be creeds if they are theologically strong enough. At ONEchapel, we try to make sure that our modern songs do reflect an important foundational truth, and we include one hymn each Sunday. We have also elected to include formal creeds, the Nicene Creed, the Apostles' Creed, the Lord's Prayer, and other foundational scriptures during our modern worship sets. Hillsong, Charles Wesley, Matt Redman, Martin Luther, and Chris Tomlin all side by side. I do not believe that "blended worship" means nobody's happy! These creeds are the way we honor our heritage and teach our young people.

CONFESSION

One of the most valuable things we do at a service is give the opportunity for people to confess their sins, receive forgiveness, and restore their relationship with God. We do this with a corporate prayer of confession, a personal examination before Communion or at the end of the service as we call people to a commitment to Christ. First John 1:9 and James 5:16 are powerful truths necessary for the people in the body of Christ to deal with sin and build community. The gospel is good news, but when we only celebrate in our services and don't leave room for reflection or confession, we minimize the work of Christ in people's hearts to rid themselves of sin and meaningfully receive forgiveness from God. Allowing people to have a moment of confession highlights this important practice and encourages it outside the service in small groups and personal relationships.

COMMUNION

At ONEchapel, we've decided to include the Lord's Table every Sunday. We participate in Holy Communion each time we gather for two reasons:

1. Jesus is the centerpiece of our worship. His death, burial, and resurrection are the focal point of Christian worship. Jesus is the demonstration of God's love to the world, and Communion helps us remember that all-important purpose for worship.

2. Communion helps us keep Christ as the center of our worship and intentionally resists the consumer mind-set that is so prevalent in our American model of church. When we take time for remembering Christ's body and blood, no matter how good the music or poor the preaching, we know we will put Christ at the center of our worship.

CANON

The Scriptures are the record of God's interaction with humanity and hold the story of God's love for our world. The God-breathed Canon holds the instructions, promises, and history of God's desire for relationship with us. Opening the Scriptures and sharing the ideas should be inspiring, challenging, and restorative as we learn to love them and live them out. My belief is that the Bible is accessible to all. At the same time, we must see the preaching and teaching of the Word through the analogy of a swimming pool. There is a deep end and a shallow end, and we must recognize that people are all over the pool. Our goal is to continually move people from the shallow end to the deep end, where they learn to swim on their own.

CONNECTION

The reason people come to church is to connect with God and with others. Everything we do in our services is targeted toward helping people experience God in a meaningful way. The presence of God is the highest priority, and so each element that we use in our services should assist in this goal. Loving God and loving people are the twin activities that accomplish God's purpose in us (Matt. 22:40). Relationships are also the conduit for ministry in the church. They are the pathway through which discipleship travels, and we must make this connection between people before we can develop their maturity. Most healthy churches have small groups, but there is also a culture created for connection in our large gatherings. Coffee, the lobby area, taking time to meet other people, greeters, name tags for everyone as they come in the door, and a conversational flow in the services are all ways that we keep people connecting at ONEchapel.

TRANSITIONING TO A FAMILY WORSHIP TABLE FORMAT

Introducing a new style of worship into your community can be difficult. But whether you are moving from traditional to modern or trying to move two or more demographically based services toward a family format, here are some ideas on what it will take.

MOVE INTENTIONALLY AND INCREMENTALLY

Change never comes quickly. Introduce new elements to your services intentionally and incrementally. Start with one element like a new hymn or chorus, or a new instrument like a guitar, or a new young person onstage. Wholesale change all at the same time is unsettling for most people. You can start with an idea like "Family Sunday," where you invite every member of the family to attend the services together and shape the services accordingly. You can invite the youth team to lead one Sunday, but then follow it up the next month with a hymn sing complete with stories of each hymn writer. In the case of a church with two different demographic services, change one element every other week for several months until both services look similar. Then, merge them together as you vision cast where you're going.

VISION CAST AND TEACH

There is no way that people will automatically love each other in a cross-generational way in church. The American church is too steeped in individualism and consumerism. You must challenge people to do it and encourage them to greater sacrifice. Share stories about an intergenerational family in your messages. Teach the ideas of family, love, and generational value in a Sunday school class, small group, or a Sunday-morning message using *Messy Church* as your workbook or text. I've heard several stories of churches that put a drum set on the stage for weeks without anyone playing it as a way of sending the message: this is where we're headed. Make sure the vision is clear and take time to say it over and over again. About the time you're sick of it, they're just getting it.

MODEL AND DISCUSS

You can't just tell the church to do it. You have to show them how to act toward one another by modeling it. Most of the time it's not the songs or the youthful graphics that attract but people. It's not changing content, it's welcoming people to contribute. If you're a church full of older people, ask some young people to help you transition and then give them a place where others can see this multi-generational approach happening—on the stage during worship, as an usher, or a greeter. If you're a young church trying to include an older demographic, invite a more mature person to give the invocation or benediction, or start a multigenerational small group with the purpose of learning from one another. Or just do any kind of project with cross-generational involvement to create a shared experience. You might assemble a multigenerational group to discuss these family ideas in order to lead the church through your transition. Be available to answer questions when church members feel insecure, and remember, actions always speak louder than words.

GET IN THE POOL!

As part of the transition, you may want to consider inviting middle-school students to "jump into" adult fellowship by not providing a separate student meeting on Sunday morning.

That is what we do at ONEchapel, and it means we have every age-group from grandparents to sixth graders represented in our gathering. This influences our language, song selections, visuals, messages and environment. The invitation of middle-school students to join "Big Church" creates an opportunity to celebrate the rite of passage for children at age twelve or thirteen to join their adult members of the family. We do this by taking time in the service to welcome students to the family table once a year on "Promotion Sunday," when most churches move every age up to the next grade. We also offer a "confirmation" type class, where students learn some of the basics of Christianity and guidelines for participating in the life of the church. Then, upon completion, we welcome them into the fellowship of adults. By doing this, we highlight the family concept for all our members and demonstrate the value we have for the youngest among us.

Remember that youth culture always moves up toward the generations before them. Young people are often the early adopters of new technology, art, and music, and therefore they influence the rest of our culture. But this is not just about culture; it's about theology as well. The family worship table reflects a spectrum of maturity in the family of God. Many have described the need to view our services like a swimming pool. There is a shallow end, a deep end, and the middle of the pool, where most people are. If the church aims for just the shallow end, mature people will be forced to simply take care of others. If the church focuses on the deep end, it's difficult for new believers to engage. My view is that we need to spend time all over the pool, not just in one section. Some services spend time in the deep end and some in the shallow end. We all understand the needs of others and so we respect them, enjoy them, and engage with them in that experience. This expresses the love that we have for one another in the family.

THE FOUR Cs OF MENTORING

1. *COACHING* FOR LIFE

Spending time with a young person so that you can give feedback and coaching through the different phases of life creates a trusting relationship. The goal of mentoring is helping a young person learn, not just from their mistakes, but also from yours. Coaching is teaching skills and training in character for success in life.

2. *CARING* FOR NEEDS

Coming to the aid of a person who is in a crisis or has a need that can only be met by someone older and wiser helps a young person feel safe. Identifying their needs even before they do with compassion and solutions creates a bond of relationship that's hard to break. Love and care are the currency of mentorship.

3. *CHALLENGING* FOR IMPROVEMENT

Zeroing in on the areas of a young person's life that they really struggle with and pushing them to change and achieve is one of the greatest contributions a mentor can make. Course correction must be done consistently to protect a young person from too great a failure, but it includes encouraging them to learn from the failures and bounce back.

4. *CHEERING* FOR CONFIDENCE

Young people need someone who will cheer them on and tell them that they can do it. Building confidence seasoned with humility is one of the primary goals for mentors who want to see a young person succeed. Cheering means identifying strengths and not just pointing out the weaknesses. It is positive reinforcement that balances out the correction and invests in the sometimes-vulnerable psyche of a young person.

Additional Resources

Sunday school materials based on family ministry:

    TRU

    tru.davidccook.com

    RIO

    rio.davidccook.com

Books:

    Think Orange by Reggie Joiner

    Collaborate: Family + Church edited by Michael
        Chanley

    Fatherless Generation by John Sowers

    Father Fiction by Donald Miller

    Shift by Brian Haynes

    When the Church Was a Family by Joseph Hellerman